P9-CQR-096

THE WIZARD OF US

THE WIZARD OF US

TRANSFORMATIONAL LESSONS FROM OZ

JEAN HOUSTON

ATRIA BOOKS
New York London Toronto Sydney New Delhi

BEYOND WORDS
Hillsboro, Oregon

ATRIA BOOKS
A Division of Simon & Schuster, Inc.
1230 Avenue of the Americas
New York, NY 10020

BEYOND WORDS
20827 N.W. Cornell Road, Suite 500
Hillsboro, Oregon 97124-9808
503-531-8700 / 503-531-8773 fax
www.beyondword.com

Copyright © 2012 by Jean Houston

All dialogue and quotes throughout this book are from the 1939 film version:
The Wizard of Oz, directed by Victor Fleming (1939; Culver City, CA: Warner Bros. Family
    Entertainment, 1999), DVD.
The Wizard of Oz music lyrics © E. Y. Harburg

All rights reserved, including the right to reproduce this book or portions thereof in any form
whatsoever without the prior written permission. For information address Atria Books/Beyond
Words Subsidiary Rights Department, 1230 Avenue of the Americas, New York, NY 10020.

The information contained in this book is intended to be educational and not for diagnosis, pre-
scription, or treatment of any health disorder whatsoever. This information should not replace
consultation with a competent healthcare professional. The content of this book is intended to be
used as an adjunct to a rational and responsible healthcare program prescribed by a professional
healthcare practitioner. The author and publisher are in no way liable for any misuse of the material.

Managing editor: Lindsay S. Brown
Editors: Emmalisa Sparrow, Anna Noak, and Gretchen Stelter
Copyeditor: Linda M. Meyer
Design: Devon Smith
Composition: William H. Brunson Typography Services

First Atria Books/Beyond Words hardcover edition November 2012

ATRIA BOOKS and colophon are trademarks of Simon & Schuster, Inc.
Beyond Words Publishing is an imprint of Simon & Schuster, Inc., and the Beyond Words logo is a
registered trademark of Beyond Words Publishing, Inc.

For more information about special discounts for bulk purchases,
please contact Simon & Schuster Special Sales at 1-866-506-1949 or
business@simonandschuster.com.

The Simon & Schuster Speakers Bureau can bring authors to your live event.
For more information or to book an event, contact the Simon & Schuster Speakers Bureau at
1-866-248-3049 or visit our website at www.simonspeakers.com.

Manufactured in the United States of America

10 9 8 7 6

Library of Congress Control Number: 2012949913

ISBN: 978-1-58270-379-4
ISBN: 978-1-4767-2840-7 (ebook)

The corporate mission of Beyond Words Publishing, Inc.: Inspire to Integrity

For Diane Nichols,
a wizard of word and laughter

CONTENTS

CONTENTS

FOREWORD

This book has a mountain to climb, and I'd like to address why the ascent is worth making. We do not believe that we live in mythic times, and we look back on such times—when knights sought the Holy Grail and Icarus flew too close to the sun—through a thick haze. Why myth? Why *bother*? At best myth flickers in and out of modern life, making it hard to tell whether a candle is sputtering out or a flame is beginning to spark.

We might think that myths are like fairy tales, enjoyed when we are children, yet left behind when the cares of adulthood force us to face hard reality. But there is another, deeper view. The most renowned expert on myth in the recent past was Joseph Campbell, who inspired readers (and millions more viewers who saw the 1988 television documentary series *The Power of Myth*) to place themselves at the center of their own personal myth. A man standing on the corner waiting for the light to turn could be the hero of a quest; a woman walking her pre-schooler to kindergarten could be expressing the eternal feminine.

No one is more capable of giving a complete narrative about myth than Jean Houston, who is passionate and astute about what myth can do. In *The Wizard of Us*, she amplifies the deeper view of myth through a virtuosic retelling of the beloved children's story *The Wizard of Oz*, using the 1939 Hollywood film version starring Judy Garland as her text. Her aim is like Campbell's; she wants the reader to see that each life has mythic value. Human beings cannot survive without meaning. Myths are the collective story of what our lives mean. As Houston says, myths are more than old tales; they are "codes and roads and maps." Where we wind up on life's journey depends on the map we carry with us.

And yet, why bother? The mountain of irrelevance towers over myth, and the reasons aren't secret. Science has triumphed as the correct way to face reality. Facts are stronger than fairy tales. The imagination cannot rival reason when it comes to making important decisions and facing new challenges. The struggle to establish science on objective findings views subjectivity as the enemy. The world "in here" is dreamy and unreliable compared to the world of matter and energy "out there." In the face of wholesale rejection, the best tactic is to co-opt our opponent. Houston joins a band of farseeing thinkers who declare that there is no split between "in here" and "out there." Reality is whole. The only issue is how you choose to explore it.

Undeniably, all of us explore it through personal experience. Our lives are occupied trying to make sense of reality, and at the heart we cannot help but follow our deep yearnings. To love and be loved fulfills one yearning, but there are others. We yearn to belong, to bond, to be safe, to feel worthwhile, to create, to express ourselves, to know the truth about God. Myth assures us that human beings have been following the same yearnings since the beginning of recorded history. What makes the mythic journey more relevant today than ever before is the hole in our lives, the void created by gazing on a universe ruled by random chance, where human existence is barely a speck in the vastness of space and time. As physics pursues its own Holy Grail, the so-called Theory of Everything that will unite the fundamental forces in Nature, it has side-stepped a Theory of Me, which would be invaluable to the doubting, seeking, confused individual.

And yet again, why bother? Why should myth fill our yearning instead of other avenues, such as organized religion? Pinning your hopes on the hero's quest isn't automatically better than pinning your hopes on faith in God. As Houston discusses so intelligently, the only reliable guide is true knowledge. Faith is what we hope to be true, which isn't the same. What myth gets at is true knowledge of the self. The self is the ultimate mystery, because no matter where you grab hold, it shifts, expands, evolves, evaporates, and leaks off into shadows down below and light up above. If myth accomplishes only one thing, it is to expose human beings as multidimensional creatures. Houston brilliantly shows that we can start anywhere, including a farmhouse in Kansas, and wind up in a transcendent world.

Truth is a word shot full of holes by skepticism. Myth lays claim to truth anyway, not because your life, and mine, is *like* a quest but because it *is* a quest. We want to write our own story, to be its author, not to be the pawn of fate, chance, or even God or the gods. No one volunteers to be insignificant. No one yearns to be powerless and without purpose. The self craves one thing: to express its potential. Looking outside ourselves, we confront limited possibilities; looking inside, the possibilities expand as far as the mind can see. From hidden, invisible possibilities, people create their life story, amalgamated from vision, dream, fear, hope, belief, desire, and expectation.

It's an unstable mixture, and there are no fixed formulas for success. When people shrug off myth (as they might shrug off art, philosophy, or spirituality) because it's too soft to be useful in a hard world, they have turned things upside down. Hard reality is fixed, resistant, unyielding, and full of obstacles. We can't penetrate it; we can only adapt to it, and probably surrender in the end. Soft reality is flexible, always changing, shaped by desire, and ruled by the mind. Soft reality is more real than hard reality. It is dynamic; it lives and grows. It takes us closer to the source, the womb of creation. Myth explains how soft reality works. It unfolds the mystery touched upon by noted physicist Freeman Dyson when he said, "I have found a universe growing without limit in richness and complexity, a universe of life surviving forever and making itself known to its neighbors across unimaginable gulfs of space and time. . . . life and intelligence can succeed in molding this universe of ours to their own purpose."[1]

There is the key: we have created a human universe. Reality is a mirror. Behind the mask of a cosmic machine whose parts can only be tinkered with, the universe is humanized. There is no other way it can exist, in fact, since nothing "out there" can be experienced except in our own consciousness. Every life story follows the trail pioneered by physicist David Bohm, among others, when he wrote, "In some sense man is a microcosm of the universe; therefore what man is, is a clue to the universe."[2] Exactly. This is a scientific way of affirming mythic truth.

In one important area Jean Houston betters Joseph Campbell—she makes myth livable. The practical side of this book lies in the Process sections of *The Wizard of Us*. To be the author of our own story, we have to get to work. The kind of work needed is inner work first, but transformation "in here" leads to results in the outer world as well.

I hope I've addressed the mountain that confronts us, and why the ascent is worth making. Jean Houston argues passionately that nothing else matters as much, since the fate of the planet depends on a collective decision. Humanity must find a way to change the narrative that currently leads to the edge of a precipice. Your art and mine is to author our own lives. Jean Houston makes the journey joyful and optimistic. In the end, will any other impulse ever arrive at the goal?

—Deepak Chopra

INTRODUCTION

Some years ago, I was sent to Taiwan on a traveling seminar with a small team sponsored by The Institute of Cultural Affairs International. We were to study the island nation's remote peoples and explore areas that few urban Taiwanese and even fewer tourists ever got to see. Surrounded by mountains, we were caught one night in a raging typhoon that seemed endless. We huddled on the slate floor of an aboriginal temple while rain dripped onto our faces through cracks in the stone roof. Great sheets of water fell from an infinite sky that had become an ocean. Lightning illuminated the dark temple every few seconds, allowing glimpses of what appeared to be shrunken heads hanging from the ceiling. (In fact, that's exactly what they were: shrunken heads.) Another flash, and a carved effigy of an ancestor loomed out of nowhere. Yet another blast of light, and a mask of demon power grimaced against the night.

My stomach was heavy with gristly snake meat. It was swimming in gluey poi paste that had been wrapped in a steamed banana leaf. The dish had been part of the festival dinner kindly offered to us by our hosts, members of the Hakka aboriginal village. They regaled us with songs and dances reminiscent of the Polynesian culture from which they were descended before coming to live in the center of Taiwan a thousand years before.

Having sought refuge with us, they explained the shrunken heads: "Oh, those are souvenirs of earlier days when we were headhunters." The last head had been acquired in World War II when a poor Japanese soldier stumbled upon their encampment, to his everlasting regret.

Incessant rain pelted the roof. In the midst of Nature's fireworks, our host declared that there was no point in trying to sleep. His grandmother, a spiritual leader of the community, sat beside him. She was a tiny woman, probably close to ninety, and a formidable presence. Her quick, little hands worked away at some beaded handicraft while her grandson translated her remarks.

"Bring in the teapot," she ordered. "This is a night for stories." She turned her matriarchal eye on me, and she commanded, "You must tell us a story from your own land."

"Uh, what kind of story would you like me to tell?" I was nervous. I could not imagine an American saga that would have any relevance to these people.

The elder conferred with her relatives. At that moment the storm got wilder. Battering rain pushed the door open, drenching those sitting near the threshold. The matriarch cackled and said, "Tell us a story about typhoons and doors that open into other worlds." Or such was the gist of the translation. I cast about in my mental library for storms and doors. With a lifetime of reading and listening to stories and myths, I found there was much from which to choose.

Just then the lightning poured forth a mighty jolt of voltage, turning Grandma into the incarnation of Mama Wizard, Mama Magus, Mama Magician. Lit up, she was the very model of an Asian Hecate, a Wizard of the East. Of course, that was it! "I will tell you the story of *The Wizard of Oz*," I announced. "The movie version," I added, for the benefit of my American companions.

Through the lightning-spattered night, drawn together against the storm, they listened, the Americans reverent before a core story of their culture, interrupting only to sing a song from the movie, the Taiwanese and the aboriginal folks adding commentary throughout. They seemed to find many correspondences between their own ancient tales and the one I was telling. Witches, good and bad, were well-known figures; the Wizard was seen as a Taoist Immortal who flew up to heaven in some magical contrivance. The lion became a dragon, and the scarecrow was assimilated into the favorite folk hero known as Monkey, while little Dorothy carried overtones of Kwan Yin.

When I finally drew to a close, intoning the great words of benediction: "There's no place like home,"* the old woman bit the thread of her beadwork, thus bringing it to a close also. Outside, Nature was silent. The windowless room was so dark we could not tell whether it was day or night. Like Dorothy, we moved to the door to see where the house had landed. And when we opened the door, we did not see rain. Blazing technicolor greeted our eyes—just like in the movie; a rendezvous of rainbows, dripping palettes of color from every tree, a world made of myth and magic. Next to me, a young member of the community attempted a little English. "There's no place like home," she said.

---

* All dialogue and quotes throughout this book are from the 1939 film version of this tale. *The Wizard of Oz*, directed by Victor Fleming (1939; Culver City, CA: Warner Bros. Family Entertainment, 1999), DVD.

"There's no place like home." What a charged and mythic phrase, innocent on the surface, but a continent loaded with possibilities when we dive deeper. "Home" is a return to what we really are—our code, our seeding, our potential destiny. How do we get there? What roads do we follow? Who has the map?

All of these codes and roads and maps are contained in the world's myths—the great stories of heroic adventures, blessed blunders, and the circle within the circles—that guides us through the maze so that we may find the deeper meaning of our lives. Myths give us the security of place and of our capacity to survive, to surmount evil, to trust in our enormous untapped potentials. They reveal to us the multidimensional universe that lies within each of us.

Let us consider the importance of *The Wizard of Oz* as a secular risen myth of North American culture and as one that has important things to tell us about our relationship to the world and our place in it. Since most people know the story in its movie form, not in its original form as the book by L. Frank Baum, I will deal largely with the movie.

Many difficulties occurred during the movie's production, including quarrels and firings and utter chaos. Margaret Hamilton as the Wicked Witch caught fire in the second take of her fiery exit from Munchkinland, and the Munchkins made rude passes at Judy Garland. Even little Terri, the dog who played Toto, caused a complete stoppage of the production when he had a nervous breakdown (and who could blame him? You've seen those flying monkeys!) But in spite of all of this, the film emerged as a pure, deep, and glorious evocation of a great story greatly told. It is a true work of art. And just as great myth is authorless, rising out of the collective unconsciousness, so the film version of *The Wizard of Oz*, with its many attempts at authorship, remains, finally, without a single author.

Something rich and strange was occurring in Hollywood studios from 1938 to 1939—active mythmaking was in progress. The latter was the greatest year of the golden age of Hollywood. And Hollywood was the mythic center of America. Some of the pictures that came out that year include: *Gone With the Wind*; *Wuthering Heights*; *Gunga Din*; *Beau Geste*; *Drums Along the Mohawk*; *Intermezzo*; *Goodbye, Mr. Chips*; *Young Mr. Lincoln*; *Mr. Smith Goes to Washington, The Women, Juarez,* and of course, *The Wizard of Oz*. All have a healthy dose of fantasy at their core; people responded to these films because of their mythic base, and also because they are essentially idealistic, not cynical. They speak to basic human needs and to where we find our substance—far more so than do films of today. These films have a sense of innocence and security, and they mirror the spirit of the country at the time. They reflect a new self-confidence after the country weathered ten years of Depression. The films of 1939 affirmed America's belief in itself and its ability to endure the emerging issues of power and plenty, or the lack thereof.

This may account for *The Wizard of Oz*'s popularity as well. Apart from being shown in movie theaters since its original release, it has been shown on television in over 900 million homes. It has an audience who can recite the dialogue and knows the songs by heart. It has become a common experience for over four generations. Popular culture is replete with references to Oz. We can find greeting cards, T-shirts, magnets, stickers, coffee mugs, cell phone ringtones, lunch-boxes, and more, all carrying images or quotes from the movie. It has become part of our collective consciousness—and because of this, it continues to speak to the deepest part of our hearts as it continues to mythologize our minds.

The Wizard of Oz is a mythic tale especially appropriate in our present time as we move into a planetary culture. There is a world mind that is rising. By that, I mean that nations can no longer afford to be islands unto themselves. The days of isolation and domination are over. We are all connected. What happens in one place quickly affects us all. In these accelerated times, we are being called to expand our ways of being; to open ourselves to the cultures of other countries; to learn as much as we can about each other and the earth itself, so we can all thrive. We stand on the brink of a new way of being that is so much more than we previously imagined.

The Wizard of Us: Traveling Mythically in Oz is a primer for training the mind to see the world in its diverse and simultaneous truths. In these chapters we identify the semiotics, or symbols, of the universal myth within. By doing so, we begin to live deliberate lives that actively connect the codes and symbols of our shared mythic story to our increased understanding of our connection to, and within, the world that now requires this shift from us.

We follow young Dorothy from Kansas down the Yellow Brick Road of the Hero's Journey. We use her heroic journey to examine the meanings of those many symbols that mark the way, and we learn to find key elements that allow us to understand where we are in our own journeys. Through our examination we learn to enhance our ability to see the layered meanings behind moments in our everyday lives and use them as touchstones to extrapolate the potentials around us. Once we begin to do that, we expand our minds and hearts, and we find the courage to create a sustainable society that works for the environment and all beings. Finally, as we answer the call to our fullest lives, we explore the ultimate questions of origin: *Who are we? Where are we going? Where do we belong? Who are we in relation to other beings? How are we being called to become our best possible selves—creators of a new way of living at this critical time?* We learn that it is possible to create a new Emerald City with all of the wonders of Oz right here on earth.

1

WE'RE OFF TO SEE THE WIZARD

We are living in the most unique time in human history. Other times in history thought they were it. They were wrong. This is it. Often our everyday, local experience is not sufficient for the enormity of the challenges that are laid upon us in this most remarkable of times. Many people have lost their belief in our economic system, our health-care system, or our educational system. The old ways of doing things are no longer working. We are now seeking the emergence of the deeper story. We are seeking our mythic lives.

Do you feel the passion within, urging you to live the greater story of your life? Myth is always about the making of the soul. It is the journey of the heroic soul as you travel from an outmoded existence to an amplified life. And in times of breakdown and breakthrough—which we're in right now—myths arise telling us of the new heroes, the new heroines, and of the noble journey we must take in search of the Possible Human both within ourselves and in others.

How do we evoke this emergence? How do we inspirit this possible, passionate human so that we may not just survive our time but thrive, leaving as our legacy a new way of being for our children, our grandchildren, and the future? It is only when we have discovered this possibility that we can go beyond our pessimism and create a world in which we make a difference.

There is an essential story, one that encompasses all the others and shows the human journey in its most complete and potent form. My old friend and colleague Joseph Campbell identified this essential story, the Hero's Journey, by studying its appearance in over 240 key stories the world over. In this book we use the term *hero* to denote both genders. Women have always been and continue to accomplish heroic feats with the difference that their emphasis has tended to be on process rather than on product—making things cohere, relate, develop, and grow. While the heroine may be less strident, she is nevertheless courageous and brings a new focus to the inner experience being of equal value to the outer action.

Campbell drew upon the vast archive of the world's stories that tell of the journey of the hero and his transformation. A pattern of details and incidents emerges from these stories. A potent similarity in theme and sequence lives within the tales of many times and cultures, showing that the world's peoples are, at our core, more alike than different.

In Campbell's book *The Hero with a Thousand Faces*,[1] we learn that all the stories ever told by oral tradition, in books, on television, and certainly in movies, have the same elements that move the story forward to a satisfying ending and make it an engaging tale that rings true in our hearts. The Hero's Journey begins with the Call to Adventure, a grand summons that beckons the hero to leave old concepts and journey forth into new ways of being. In most cases, the hero is a reluctant hero in that he or she is going about his or her normal life at the beginning of the story and suddenly the everyday world is thrown radically out of balance. In *The Wizard of Oz*, Dorothy is called to a larger life beyond her outmoded situation.

You may have already felt this Call to Adventure in your own life. Now that you have experienced it, with all its triumphs and disasters, shadows and glory, you may find yourself awaiting a different kind of call. A call perhaps from the earth herself and her people, the hounds of heaven barking at your heels, calling you to make a difference in the world.

The next stage in Campbell's cycle of the Hero's Journey is the Refusal of the Call: putting off the summons or delaying it because it comes at an inconvenient time or because you don't feel yourself worthy. The regular job, the regular paycheck, the habitual routines and their drugs of fatigue and futility can all inhibit the call. You find that you can keep refusing the call until you can't stand yourself anymore. You can refuse the call, but something will keep reminding you, needling you until you step into your destiny.

Once the hero accepts the call, he or she receives special aid on the adventure from magical allies who help the hero make important decisions along the path. In the case of *The Wizard of Oz*, Dorothy accepts the call, finds herself in Oz, and meets magical allies in the form of Glinda, the Good Witch of the North; the Scarecrow; the Tin Man; and the Cowardly Lion.

On her path, the hero next comes to the Guardian of the Threshold. This is often a typically unfriendly monster given to schedules, fixed habits, and attitudes cast in stone. A worthy adversary, the guardian often shows up in everyday life as a supervisor or boss or an unsolicited advisor who follows the status quo. At worst, this guardian metaphorically (or literally, in the movies) devours the hero or turns the hero into a wimpy version of herself. At best, the guardian hones the hero's pluck and cunning and requires that she engage the guardian in witty banter in order to get past the dangers. This is where the hero learns to think outside of the box. This is also the point where the hero actually crosses into the field of adventure, leaving the known limits of his or her world behind, and ventures into an unknown realm of amplified power. In traditional journeys, this stage involves leaving the world of ordinary reality and entering the inner, visionary realms where the rules and limits are unknown. In our story, this realm is Oz.

Once across the threshold, our hero reaches the Belly of the Whale. He or she is swallowed by the unknown, be it a whale, a wolf, or a cave. This is where the hero lets go of old habits that are no longer useful. Old conditioning is released in order for the hero to be rewoven into a stronger and brighter form. The Belly of the Whale can appear in many guises in our real lives. It can take the form of a depression or introversion or even a strong need to get away from it all.

The Belly of the Whale represents the final separation from the hero's known world and known self. It is sometimes described as the person's lowest point, but it is actually the point at which the hero is between or is transitioning between worlds and selves. The separation has been made, or is being made, or is being fully recognized between the old world and old self and the potential for a new world and new self. By entering this stage of the journey, our hero shows a willingness to undergo a metamorphosis or even the death of the old self in order to emerge as a new being.

Now our hero comes to the Road of Trials along the Hero's Journey. This is a time of incredible tests and extraordinary adventures! Campbell told us that this is where "the hero moves in a dream landscape of curious fluid, ambiguous forms, where he must survive a succession of trials."[2] Generally, this sequence is the favorite of story-tellers, epic poets, and novelists, for it is here that they give full vent to the dread we all feel before the unknown and the unbound, be it in desert, wilderness, or sea, or in the corresponding places in the labyrinth of our own unconscious life. Our hero is hurled into adventures and challenges for which she has had little preparation and yet somehow finds the resources to survive. The hero's magical helpers and supernatural allies help out on the Road of Trials.

The next stage of the journey brings the hero to the deepest stage of the cycle, where a Father/Creator character, also known as the Presence, recognizes him. The hero achieves a sacred marriage with a spiritual form or inner beloved of the soul and enters his apotheosis or transformation.

It has been said that the Meeting with the Beloved represents the point in the adventure when the hero experiences a love that has the power and significance of the all-powerful, all-encompassing, unconditional love that a fortunate infant may experience with his or her mother. It is also known as the *hieros gamos*, or sacred marriage, the union of opposites, and may take place entirely within the person. In other words, the person begins to see herself in a nondualistic way. This is a very important step in the process of the Hero's Journey and is often represented by the hero finding the other person that he or she loves most completely. Although Campbell described the symbolism of this step as a meeting with a goddess, unconditional love and self-unification do not have to be represented by a man or a woman.

In fact, Campbell offered us an alternative way to meet the demands of this stage of the adventure: stealing or acquiring a boon or favor for which we are questing. This has taken many, many forms: an elixir of life, the fire of immortality, the key to knowledge, the ring of power, the philosopher's stone—in other words, some big-time reward. "Intrinsically," Campbell wrote, "it is an expansion of consciousness and therein of being."[3] In the case of our friends in Oz, the Wizard grants the boons of a brain, a heart, courage, and a way home, but as we all know from the film, Dorothy and her allies discover that they had these attributes all along, they only needed to believe in themselves to discover their many latent talents and powers.

Once the boon is granted, our hero is ready for the magical flight back across the threshold with the boon intact, so that with it, he or she may restore the world. At this moment in the Hero's Journey, our hero becomes the Master of Two Worlds, able to bring the greening power of the depth world into the graying world of ordinary space and time. This certainly is the case with Dorothy Gale when she returns as a fully empowered and activated hero at the end of *The Wizard of Oz*. In your case, you may find new reserves of inner strength and the passion for the possible. You may find the ability to become strongly related to ideas that you love and cherish, to appreciate what you have created, and to have the gift of sustaining that appreciation over time.

We are all on a Hero's Journey. We have all experienced a Call to Adventure. We have all lived through a Belly of the Whale experience. You don't have to be Hercules or Achilles, Odysseus or Perseus to be a hero. Consider the power you exercise right here, right now. You have the capacity to do some good in the world, to do brilliant, beautiful things. However, you may not know this, or you may forget what you are capable of during the stress of the everyday world. Any one of us born in this scientific age of quantum realities recognizes that we are all every part of every story. You may realize that you are both the storyteller and the story itself. So, what story are you telling? What story are you being? We take a look at the stages of our own lives as we move along this Hero's Journey with Dorothy.

Myth is the loom on which we may weave our own journey of transformation. I find that regardless of whatever culture I'm working with, people grow further and faster in both their human and their social potentials if there is a story or myth attached to the work. That is because we are the living, breathing connection between the great stories that speak to what is deep and eternal in us, and the playing out of these stories in real life. Each part of any myth offers opportunities to weave physical, mental, psychological, and spiritual growth, thus enabling us to move much more fully through these dimensions of the self. Growth in body, mind, and psyche allows you to enter the larger story of our world, as well as your own story.

Myth speaks to all conditions. It transcends time, place, gender, job, and status. Working with myth in a creative manner can provide us with fresh perspectives on our life journey. It can take us beyond our ordinary, habitual ways of being to the essence of who and what we really are or can be.

In myths ancient and modern, we travel into deeper parts of ourselves. We explore magic with Merlin, fight for the good with Wonder Woman, become Isis seeking Osiris, and even join the Starship *Enterprise* crew in seeking out new worlds and galaxies. We experience epic challenges in space with Prince Leia, quest for the Grail with Percival, descend into the underworld with Inanna, and voyage with Odysseus. We assume the passion and pathos of Psyche and Eros, Romeo and Juliet; we search for the Beloved of the Soul with the lovers who inhabit the mythic universe.

All the complexities of our shadowed selves are also represented—by the great villains of the mythic universe: Mordred, Darth Vader, wicked stepmothers, Voldermort, and the indifferent gods of chaos. Gradually, we discover that their stories are our own stories. They bear the amplified rhythms of our own unique local life, and by touching into them, we touch into the larger frequency, the larger rhythms, the larger life. Mythic kingdoms thrive inside of you, their societies intact. Think of Arthurian Camelot. Can you almost feel the reverberation of that great civilization that continues to arise in you?

These mythic characters, themes, and whole societies within give us their power, their prestige, their tragedy and comedy, and their resurrection. Chances are you have experienced this in your own life. Have you ever been like Romeo or Juliet, madly in love? Or Hercules, performing one arduous task after another? Have you been Yoda, with the wisdom that he imparts? They're all there. Having lived through Joan of Arc, Rumi White Buffalo Calf Woman, or little Dorothy, we return to our own lives deepened and enhanced. We discover that we live in a greater universe with larger potentials, capacities that transcend and invigorate us beyond the potentials we learned in our local lives, fine as they may be.

What you see in *The Wizard of Oz* is not only myth but also a powerful initiatory drama of the Hero's Journey. Explicitly, it is about Dorothy's initiatory rite of passage from her home in Kansas, through the deep, archetypal world of Oz with all that she learns there, and her return to Kansas. Implicitly, however, it is about Dorothy's rite of passage from childhood, through the perils of adolescence. Dorothy goes home to Kansas, but not before she grows up in Oz. Not before she discovers her own world of sufficiency and abundance. It is in Oz that she undergoes the great Road of Trials that teaches her about discovering the riches and uses of one's full intelligence, friendship, and compassion. She also learns about the genius of working in partnership with others and how the committed community can do almost anything. Finally, she learns about the magic, the wizardry, the sacred potency that lies within each of us, even though we may initially fear it or see it as pointless, but eventually accept and appreciate it. The movie ends where it begins, in Kansas. Dorothy has gone home, but she is changed; she has grown, deepened. Although she feels she can find everything in her own backyard, we in the audience know that the backyard contains the vaster domains of her own subconscious mind, and quite possibly the collective unconscious of the human race and the planetary mind as well. Dorothy returns mythic, and we know that she will green the wasteland of Kansas with her newfound knowings. Indeed, the subsequent books in the Oz series state just that; they open up a bridge between two worlds that is constantly available. That is the power of myth. It is deep. It allows us to be more.

Let's take a brief look at the person who brought this story out of the ether and onto the page. L. Frank Baum (1856–1919) wrote *The Wonderful Wizard of Oz* in 1900. The book became an instant success. However, Baum's personal Road of Trials was a long and arduous one, spanning decades of failure after failure in business, as well as a fair amount of personal heartache. In fact, one could certainly say that Baum lived a mythic life while traveling his own Hero's Journey. His tenacity and overall optimistic attitude are inspirational for those of us who may think we have it rough sometimes.

In the enlightening biography on Baum's life, *The Real Wizard of Oz* by Rebecca Loncraine, we learn much about the "man behind the curtain."[4] In 1898 Baum got a flash of inspiration about a little girl swept from her home in Kansas by a fearsome tornado and plunked down in a magical land filled with wonders. The author claimed that the idea came to him whole and all at once, as though it had been there all along, waiting for him to discover it. (This story was corroborated by Baum's great-granddaughter in a personal email to me.) "Frank Baum, who wrote the story entirely by hand with a pencil, said that 'the tale came easily, as if it were being written through him.'"[5]

To make sure that children responded favorably to various aspects of the story, he would often test his ideas on kids in his neighborhood in an animated fashion that drew upon all of his acting and storytelling skills. As the story goes, Baum was telling the tale of Dorothy, the Scarecrow, the Tin Man, and the Cowardly Lion to a group of children in his study one afternoon when a child asked where all these fascinating creatures lived. What was the name of the place? Baum's gaze fell upon a file cabinet across the room with drawers marked *A–N* and *O–Z*. And his answer, of course, was "Oz!"[6]

Baum was pleased with this new work and on December 31, 1899, he had a finished manuscript of his latest achievement: *The Emerald City*. The title was soon changed because of a superstition held by publishers that any book with a jewel mentioned in the title would never be successful,[7] and after sifting through many other possibilities, the title *The Wonderful Wizard of Oz* won out. The book was dedicated to his faithful, loving wife, Maud, who had stuck with her hard-working husband through the good times and the numerous challenging times—the one who had believed in him and encouraged his imagination all along the way.

It is interesting to note that this book was completed just as one century ended and another began, much like the energy of the current time in which we find ourselves. Our world is on the brink of great transformation, and Baum's simple, yet powerful multilayered, mythic story has emerged once again to guide us.

Baum and a talented illustrator, William Wallace Denslow, pooled their resources to partially pay for publication of the novel, which was beautifully illustrated in full color. It was a risk. In her children's biography of Baum's life, Kathleen Krull wrote:

Frank's first clue about how his risk would pay off came near Christmas. The Baums were out of money again. Maud insisted that he stop by his publisher's office to ask for some—even one hundred dollars would be a help. So he did. The publisher wrote him a check and he stuck it in his pocket without looking at it. Back at home, Maud was ironing shirts. The legend is that she asked for the money and then dropped the iron and burned a hole in the shirt. (The check was for several thousand dollars.)[8]

Frank Baum's years of struggle finally paid off. *The Wonderful Wizard of Oz* was a tremendous success when it came out. Since its first publication, it has been translated into multiple languages across the globe and remains one of the best-loved creations in all of children's literature to this day.

In bringing us the rich and vibrant world of Oz, L. Frank Baum truly lived out and immortalized his own Hero's Journey, creating a world of endless possibility all around us. In his time he wrote fifty-five novels, eighty-two short stories, over two hundred poems, and many scripts, often attempting to bring his work to stage and screen. His imaginative works predicted such amazing inventions as cell phones, laptop computers, and television.

Can you imagine that there was a time before there existed a Cowardly Lion or a Tin Man or a Scarecrow in search of a brain? Before Dorothy of Kansas and her little dog Toto made the fabled trip to a place called Oz? Of course you can't, for the entire Land of Oz leapt from Frank Baum onto the page as a download so complete and real that none of us doubt its existence. Because one man made the trip to discover a Yellow Brick Road and an Emerald City, we may all travel there whenever we like. Indeed we may learn to create an Emerald City of infinite possibility all around us.

Since the book's release, the effect of *The Wonderful Wizard of Oz* has been like a force field illuminating whoever or whatever comes its way. When the story entered the cinema in Technicolor in 1939 as the abbreviated *Wizard of Oz*, laced with catchy songs and filled with soul by sixteen-year-old Judy Garland and her voice of pure plums (that's the only way I can describe her voice), it became an American cultural myth invested with the power to cause its audience to enter a different reality.

It is a story we remember, believe, and cherish in our hearts. To each generation, the story rises and blooms anew in the psyche. It is a story invested with all of our potentials and highest ideals, as well as our shadows and terrors. It speaks to the basic human need for companionship. It is innocent and sincere. As it remembers a golden age in our agrarian past, it simultaneously portrays a technological golden age in the immediate future. We find the security of place, the assurance that we have in us a sufficiency of capacities to confront evil and survive, and the ability to trust in our own enormous untapped potentials. Then, like Dorothy, we can come back and re-green the wasteland, the Kansas of our lives. We *are* Oz. In any mythic structure we may identify with the hero, but in truth we contain all of the characters. Dorothy might be any one of us. Or we might be the Tin Man in our longing to feel loving connections, the Scarecrow seeking our true intelligence, or the Cowardly Lion seeking courage. We contain the Great and Powerful Wizard. What would happen if we dared to dip into this high and holy magic within ourselves?

Like all great stories, *The Wizard of Oz* provides a template that allows us to open ourselves to the hidden capacities we had forgotten we had; the creative potentials we didn't know how to use; and the deeper knowing that transcends past, present, and future—a deeper knowing that is within every one of us. We are so much more than we thought we were. This magical movie speaks to our bodies, our minds, our spirits so as to bring the fullness of who and what we are, the required humans, fully capable of cocreating a better society, as is seen in the Emerald City.

In the pages that follow, we see how the tale follows the stages of the Hero's Journey. There is a wasteland—Kansas—in the beginning of the story. There is tremendous yearning. There's a heroic little girl who's called to redeem the time, to make life work. And like the hero, she's stopped at every turn. Have you ever been stopped at every turn, ignored, made to appear foolish, put down? Nothing is working in her life or has any positive energy but her little dog, and even Toto is being threatened with death by nasty Miss Gulch.

Through the vehicle of a twister, she crosses the threshold of space and time into a realm of amplified power, as the hero does. There she meets allies as well as shadow creatures. She undergoes trial and transformation. She gains the pearl, at great price, of self-knowing, which she then brings home in order to positively transform the wasteland of her regular life.

Like all great myths, *The Wizard of Oz* doesn't stay static; it grows and adds new dimensions, subtracts outmoded forms, and is altogether an evolutionary event. We see something that was known but not recognized by previous generations: racial interspecies reality. Here are four characters who are species varied: a young girl, a tin man who could double as a robot, a talking lion who is also a great clown, and a dancing scarecrow. The animal, vegetable, mineral, and human kingdoms are all there together. It's about total ecology across the great reality spectrum.

These four wildly different beings skip, arm in arm, down the Yellow Brick Road, the road of spiritual pollen. That they do so speaks to our hopes for a truly integrated society—a world that honors the diversity of many cultures, as well as the culture of the earth. That's why it's such an extraordinary story. The movie version of the story has emerged as a very rich, deep, and glorious evocation of a powerful journey splendidly told. This, then, is our story, and woven around this story is the story of a life—Dorothy's life, my life, your life.

13

2

JOURNEY OF THE COMPASSIONATE HERO

Compared to the hundreds of mythic stories that Joseph Campbell studied in order to develop his structure of the Hero's Journey, the story of Dorothy and *The Wizard of Oz* is unique. Perhaps influenced by his wife and mother-in-law, L. Frank Baum believed in the rights of women and favored strong female protagonists in his books. Unlike tales of mighty men who began as reluctant heroes only to accept the call to adventure and then find themselves hacking through forests filled with Orcs and goblins to arrive atop a mountain of dead enemies, bloody swords drawn in triumph, Dorothy is a compassionate hero.

While the male heroes who populate mythic tales from all times and lands take on the world and bend civilizations to do their bidding, Dorothy only wants to return home. And her longing for home has less to do with returning to the Great Depression–era, black-and-white dustbowl of Kansas and the meager living she might eventually eke out as a farmer's wife than with returning home to save her Auntie Em, whom she believes is heartbroken because of her disappearance.

Indeed, every step along the Yellow Brick Road is paved with Dorothy's inner strength, spirit of love, and compassion for others. Unlike many male heroes who might chuckle in triumph while wrenching the valuable ruby slippers from the cold, dead feet of the Wicked Witch of the East—after having first dropped a house on her—Dorothy is horrified to discover that she has accidentally caused the witch's demise. It would never have occurred to the girl to steal the magic slippers.

Compassion spurs Dorothy to pry the Scarecrow from his wooden perch and to oil the rusted Tin Man. Love and kindness prompt her to ask her first two allies to join her on the road to meet the Wizard so that they might be granted the brain and the heart they so deeply desire. When the Cowardly Lion attacks her little dog Toto, it is her courage that allows her to defend her tiny pooch with a well-placed slap to the lion's nose. She does not act with a desire to be aggressive or dominate—only with care and protection of her beloved companion. Dorothy solves problems by using her natural, nurturing qualities. Even when faced with the formidable Wicked Witch of the West, it is Dorothy's love and compassion for the Scarecrow, whose arm has been lit afire by the witch, that causes her to throw the bucket of water that puts out the fire and thus accidentally melts the evil creature on the spot.

Unlike the male heroes in many tales who steal the boon that allows them access to two worlds, Dorothy is handed the witch's broomstick as a trophy by the Leader of the Guards. She is given the boon freely, in gratitude, because she has freed the soldiers who had been held in servitude by the witch.

This idea of a heroine approaching the challenges of her journey in a different way from that of traditional male heroes is another reason why a closer examination of this particular story is so perfect for our present time and situation in history. New ways of thinking are being called forth. The old methods of "conquer and destroy" are ineffective and outdated. Aspects of the Divine Feminine energy are rising up and sliding into more of a partnership with Divine Male energy as our world moves toward a necessary, more ideal planetary balance.

The original book *The Wonderful Wizard of Oz* opens with the description of Dorothy's world of Kansas. As far as the eye can see, there is nothing but the gray, bleak landscape of the prairie, a failed wasteland. Even the house where little Dorothy lives is gray. As for Auntie Em, as L. Frank Baum described her, "The sun and wind had taken the sparkle from her eyes and left them a sober gray; they had taken the red from her cheeks and lips, and they were gray also. She was thin and gaunt, and never smiled now." And "Uncle Henry never laughed. He was gray also, from his long beard to his rough boots."[1] The sky on the day in which the miracle of translation to another realm is about to happen was "even grayer than usual." Toto, the positive, energetic life force, represented by a silky, little brown dog, is the positive influence that saves Dorothy from growing as gray as her surroundings. This is the utter realization of the wasteland that we all face sometime in our lives—a gray landscape with gray adults doing their work without joy.

In the movie, the theme of the gray world is developed further. The scenes of the Dust Bowl–era Kansas farm are shown in geometric lines, with telegraph poles, fences, and triangular houses placed against a vast emptiness. It is a broken, abandoned, impoverished world. Dorothy bursts onto this scene talking a mile a minute to her Auntie Em and Uncle Henry about the upsetting event that just occurred between her dog and mean old Miss Gulch. The old couple, however, are engaged in a task of dull arithmetic—counting their chicks, a source of their small income. Through numbers and simple shapes, the family defends itself against the bleak emptiness of Kansas. The sense of scarcity is what makes up their entire world. There is no generosity here; they will not even take the time to respond to Dorothy in any way. Counting chickens is more important than listening to one's own children, as if counting were the measure of morality, goodness, and soul. Adults stay helpless and children go unnourished.

How many parents in our own time relate to their children in sound bites and expect them to be quiet and stay out of the way? A good many members of the baby boom generation fit this description, as do children who grow up in the urban wastelands of concrete lined with bullet casings. People in the wasteland give up on their children and themselves. They fall asleep because they cannot see beyond their gray condition. The difference is that in this story—and in your story, too—there is still one person awake. One person is still alive to the dream. Dorothy must not sit in her room and wait but must go somewhere, because she is called. And you are called as well. Think for a minute about how you have been called to leave the wasteland and find a better life.

Dorothy tries again to get someone to listen to her by turning to the farmhands, but it becomes quickly apparent that they are as helpless as she is. When she walks along the fence rail surrounding the pigsty, she tumbles in and has to be rescued. Auntie Em admonishes her, "You always get yourself in a fret over nothing. Find yourself a place where you won't get into any trouble." There it is—the invitation into the myth, the call to adventure. She asks Toto if there is such a place, affirming that "there must be." She sings "Over the Rainbow," the song that has become the beautiful anthem to the search for a deeper, truer reality. As Salman Rushdie said, "Judy Garland gave the film its heart."[2] Indeed, when we hear the yearning in Judy Garland's voice as her face lifts to the skies, we understand what Rushdie means when he said:

What she expresses here, what she embodies with the purity of an archetype, is the human dream of leaving—a dream at least as powerful as its countervailing dream roots. At the heart of *The Wizard of Oz* is a great tension between these two dreams; but, as the music swells and that big, clean voice flies into the anguished longings of the song, can anyone doubt which message is stronger? In its most potent emotional moment, this is inarguably a film about the joys of going away, of leaving grayness and entering the color, of making a new life in the place where you won't get into any trouble.[3]

Imagine that scene that is forever impressed in our minds—the image of Dorothy and Toto, their heads lifted toward the sky, invoking the great beyond, the higher self, the realm beyond the rainbow where the archetypes dwell. What Dorothy is expressing is the pure archetypal human dream of going into another realm, a dream that is as powerful as the countervailing dream of returning home. At the heart of *The Wizard of Oz* is the tension between the two heroic dreams of leaving and returning.

Looking into the gray sky, she can see the "perhaps" realm so clearly, even envisioning its future colors where skies are blue and the "dreams that you dare to dream really do come true."[4] As Dorothy sings, she is coded with new possibilities and brought to a state of ripening so the new reality can take place.

Think of rainbows you have seen and what they called up in you. We live within a time in which people of many colors and colorful cultures are in search of putting ourselves all together in a beautiful and brilliant way—a rainbow of peoples. Once we do it, it will be a totally different society, an illumination of the earth.

Rainbows in sacred and mythic literature are always signs from the realm of the divine: Noah knows that the world will begin anew when he sees the rainbow; the Peacemaker in the Iroquois legend can foretell in the rainbow the coming of a new society; and, of course, there is always that pot of gold at the end of the rainbow. Rainbows are associated with the golden age when earth and heaven were in easy communication—deities, angels, and mortals passing back and forth on the rainbow bridge. This reminds us that within the rainbow itself there are not just seven colors but spectrums of color invisible to the naked eye; the rainbow beyond the rainbow, calling us to domains and dimensions that are not yet visible. Consider, too, the shape of the rainbow—it is a U-turn. It's not only a going outward but a coming back, not only an inward turning but a going forth, a traveling to Oz and a returning home to our own backyard.

Most important, rainbows cause us to wish, to yearn, to dream. Just think about what happened to you when you failed to dream, or when your dream was stunted and not large enough to get you going. To have a good dream is to be charged from the deeper reality to go about your sacred business. A good dream is a message from the Universe. It pulls you from one world into another and keeps you constantly charged to go out beyond habits, contexts, and traditions to make things happen. Dorothy has heard the call, felt the longing. She is coded with the new possibility. Once you say yes to the dream, circumstances conspire to test you and offer you opportunities to make the new reality happen. So, of course, Dorothy's situation gets darker.

Evil arrives in the form of Miss Gulch (played to perfection by Margaret Hamilton, who also plays the Wicked Witch of the West), a singularly small-minded person and the richest woman in town. Her narrow features match her narrow vision of the world. Dorothy's initial predicament is how to battle the ravenous appetite of this angry woman, whose power and wealth threaten to engulf the young girl and her family. Miss Gulch has arrived on her bicycle in a fury, threatening to take away the last vestige of innocent spirit, the little dog Toto, whom she claims bit her. She produces an injunction from the local sheriff giving her permission to take the dog and have him "destroyed." Dorothy watches in despair as the woman roughly shoves the dog into a basket that she straps onto the back of her bicycle and wheels away.

Things look bleak. Dorothy feels helpless and hopeless, faced with a situation over which she has no control. Naturally, Toto (who is very clever) escapes and scampers home to the girl. Nuzzling him, she tearfully realizes that nothing will change unless she does something radically different, something unthinkable. Feeling that her only option is to take her beloved dog and run away, she stuffs a few possessions into a bag and rushes out the door.

As dark clouds gather in the distance, Dorothy hurries down the dusty road and stops at the encampment of Professor Marvel (the amazing Frank Morgan who plays five roles in the film, including Professor Marvel and the Wizard himself), a traveling roadside gypsy, a haphazard magician of sorts who is toasting weenies over an open fire. Toto knows instinctively that the benign Professor Marvel is really a very great man in disguise; thus, where Toto earlier bites Miss Gulch on the leg, now he takes a bite out of the Professor's hot dog. The Professor finds this amusing. Dorothy begs to run away with the man because she wants to visit all of the crowned heads of Europe, as his painted wagon suggests he does. He notices her satchel and begins to speak intuitively to her, saying in a semihypnotic voice, "They don't understand you at home. They don't appreciate you. You want to see other lands, big cities, big mountains, big oceans." He guesses at the deeper, underlying reason for her unhappiness: that she is longing for the journey that gives us the training and initiation into the next level of being.

"Why, it's just like you could read what was inside of me," she replies. She is ready to explore new terrain, go to geographical and psychological locales she has never been to before.

Professor Marvel offers to read her fortune in a crystal ball, a talent he swears was passed on to him from the days of Isis and Osiris. This traveling man has spent much of his life on the road selling snake oil, a little magic, a lot of hooey, and much common sense. Even though on the surface he may appear to be a scam artist, the truth is that he has traveled the human heart as well as country roads, and this has given him a lot of wisdom about people. With age has come more compassion, and he feels for this child who yearns as much as he yearned long ago in his own youth. This sensitive shaman has invented his scallywag profession in order to practice real healing and the empowerment of those who might otherwise be discounted. He asks her to close her eyes to "go inward," and when she does so, he peers into her bag to find the photograph of Auntie Em, whom he then "clairvoyantly" describes as looking for Dorothy, clutching her heart, which sends the girl rushing home. This is, however, a false return. Dorothy is on the initiatory path, the path of redeeming the higher dream, and therefore she needs something extraordinary to happen to keep her on her path so that she might re-green the land and the heart.

In the Hero's Journey, this discovery of a lower path and a higher path are important to the hero's eventual acceptance of the Call to Adventure. Once this threshold has been passed, the hero is on his way into an entirely new world with new rules. The reality he has known before falls away.

Process: Seeing Yourself as the Hero of Your Own Journey

Where are you on the path of the Hero's Journey? Oftentimes, we find ourselves experiencing several aspects of the journey all at the same time. Take a moment to see yourself as the hero. Where are you? What are you wearing? What are you holding? Get out a pencil, a pen, or some crayons, and draw yourself as the hero. You may feel intimidated by this activity, but I would urge you to draw when prompted since drawing activates a part of the brain that perhaps is not used regularly. There is no need for you to be a Rembrandt! No one will see your work unless you allow it, and doing these exercises as they are written expands your skill sets. So grab your drawing materials and let your inspiration guide you as you create yourself writ large. What magical attributes do you have?

Imagine yourself as the hero poised in the middle of the page, as if suspended by the force of a tornado. Look down at the black-and-white farm fields of Kansas below you. What do you want to let go of from your outmoded past or from the present that no longer serves you? Let those things go. Let go of that job that no longer serves you. Let go of relationships that no longer serve you. Let go of your own limitations. Let go and watch them drift away into the black-and-white world below. Draw those things that you are ready to let go of.

Now what would you like to draw *to* you in a life of infinite possibilities? Look up into the Technicolor dream world of Oz. It is a place where anything is possible. Draw the things you wish to attract to yourself across the top of the paper. There's that new job where you are well paid and appreciated for your talents. There's that new relationship. There's the ability to make the world a better place. As you imagine those things that you wish to attract to you, draw them on the paper. You are Dorothy, accepting the call and stepping into the great Hero's Journey.

Back in Kansas, the storm has now become full-blown, and the girl finds herself racing down the road with the tornado right behind her, scouring the already bleak landscape with its black funnel. To Dorothy's right and left, trees are ripped from the ground; the gate is difficult to open with the force of the wind. Auntie Em, Uncle Henry, and the three farmhands must now take cover. Auntie Em screams for Dorothy but, alas, the farmhands push her into the cellar just as the girl arrives.

Leaning against the wind, the desperate girl struggles to open the gate leading to her yard. She manages to open the screen door to the main house, and the door immediately rips from its hinges and blows away. Dorothy dashes madly through the house, opening doors that then slam shut and trying to reopen them. She runs outside and pounds on the cellar door, but it is tightly closed and no one hears her. She moves quickly back into the house, back into what she hopes is the familiar shelter of her room, calling feebly for Auntie Em. Suddenly, a window blows out of its casing and hits her on the head. She spins and falls into an altered state of consciousness—the state that generally attends many, if not most, rites of passage. This is the final gateway. The spiraling tornado is seen through the window and everything begins to twist and turn.

Tornados are fascinating. Before they descend, there is a period of incredible stillness, as if nothing were ever going to change. No wind. The light is almost green, and the sky is bathed in incredible colors that don't seem to appear anywhere else in nature until that moment of the twister. Then, from a long way off, there is a roar, a dull, dimly perceived sound. Huge piles of clouds appear in various shades of black and gray, some with a morbid, bluish tinge. Together, they are the grim reaper of the sky. Then the tail of the tornado appears, and you can see it snaking its way along, a gourmand of landscapes. It sucks and gobbles cornfields and houses, ripping and tearing and chewing.

The amazing thing about twisters is that they have the capacity to send a single straw to pierce the body of a tree and also lift up entire houses and cattle and set them down miles away without harm. The twister is a wild card, nature's deviant talent. Afterward, there is a concerted effort of rebuilding as the towns and their societies are re-formed. People are called to do things they have never done before, sometimes moving from being a mere neighbor to being a rescuer, from "just a guy down the street" to a giver of blood and a lifeline to others. A tornado changes people. It shakes us up and makes us better.

We are currently living in twister times, when everything is flying apart out of the sheer excessive charge of the winds of change. Migrants are pouring across borders, governments are dissolving, financial institutions are crumbling, media is connecting people at warp speed, weather is going berserk, and no one and nothing is able to avoid any of this anymore. The collective doors are off their hinges and we have fallen through into a world that we do not know and never suspected existed. What is more, the global twister is twisting new strands into human nature from the codings that lay dormant within us. It's the breakdown of the membrane and the breakthrough of the depths.

What emotional or psychological twisters have you brought on yourself in order to get away from your "Kansas?" Marriage? Divorce? Illness? Going broke? Gaining weight or getting too skinny? Dropping out? Getting yourself into interesting "adventures?" Like Dorothy, taking on a twister is what human beings often do to get themselves from here to there. And sometimes twisters simply arrive on their own steam. It comes with the territory of being an earthling.

Just as *The Wizard of Oz* takes place during the Great Depression in America, a time when people were living in survival mode, so we find ourselves today in a time of radical change, of wondering if we'll lose our jobs, our traditional ways of doing things, our grasp on the reality we have known. Many of the outmoded beliefs that have defined us as individuals and as a country seem to be flying away on the winds of change. In times when we are in survival mode, we cannot look up to see the spiritual world that surrounds us.

There is a psychological theory by Abraham Maslow, which is commonly called Maslow's Hierarchy of Needs.[5] Maslow is known as the leader of the humanist school of psychology. His theory describes the various stages of human growth and is often represented by a pyramid. The base of the pyramid focuses on the most fundamental human needs such as our need for air to breathe, water, food, and shelter. People who are just barely getting by are operating at the base level of the pyramid. When a person is operating at this level, she is only concerned with survival. There's no time or energy left over to worry about higher pursuits such as creativity and art or, say, following a spiritual path, when a person doesn't know where the next meal is coming from. The focus is on staying alive.

Maslow suggested that these most basic of human needs must first be met before a person can move upward on the pyramid. He also noticed that some people have a stronger drive to go beyond the scope of fundamental needs in order to strive for something better. He called this *Metamotivation*. Once a person's physical needs are met, he moves up to Safety Needs. These have to do with the human need for our environment to be predictable and orderly. In the professional arena of a person's life, there is some sort of job security, health insurance, and maybe a savings plan. This level of the pyramid has to do with personal security, financial security, health, and well-being.

Once the basic survival needs and security needs are met, people move up to a Social Level. Here they can afford to breathe easily enough to look for some sense of belonging. This is hardwired into our brains, not only because there is safety in numbers but because the human animal has existed in tribes since there have been bipedal hairless apes walking around on this planet. Maslow's hierarchy on this level includes friendship and its balm for loneliness. It includes intimacy, sharing, and, ultimately, family.

At the core of every one of us is the need to belong and to be accepted by our peers. We all want to belong to and be a part of something, whether it's at the office, at church, on sports teams, in clubs, or, especially, in families. So, Maslow told us, once we have air to breathe, water to drink, food to eat, clothes to wear, a place to sleep with a roof over our heads, and some way to make a living, we feel safe enough to open up to others, and the first thing we strive for is connection. We all want to be loved, and we all want to belong.

The fourth level is concerned with Esteem—the need to be accepted and valued by others. We enter into activities that offer a sense of contribution and value that give back to the community in some way.

Finally, the top tier of Maslow's pyramid is the need for Self-Actualization. It is here that a person steps into her full potential. Society's restrictive suit of conformity is stripped away. Though we must still live in the world, we don't need to be of the world, as Dorothy soon discovers.

At this level, having risen above the lower levels by mastering them, we find the freedom to express creative ideas through art, poetry, and music. This is the realm of invention and imagination. It is also where we may attain the realization that we are made of God stuff, that we are not separate from the Creator.

As a very young person, I was befriended by Abe Maslow and used to challenge him on his hierarchy, pointing out that there were people living at the lowest levels of survival and yet functioning creatively at the highest levels. I further argued that perhaps we could turn the hierarchy into a circle wherein the different stages had access to each other rather than the needs of each being constrained by a particular level. In his final days, Maslow wrote me a long letter in which he asked me to explore my idea further. Having subsequently worked in some 108 countries, and often among the poorest of people, I have seen such creativity and soulful action on the part of women and men living in the most abject of circumstances. Out of misery has been born song, dance, innovative social projects, and grappling with challenges equal to anything Dorothy and her allies met on their journey. The wisdom that these seeming unfortunates express, their conversations and good humor, are a testament to the resilience of the human condition. Therefore, although I do not deny the general truth of Maslow's theory, I do believe that my experience suggests that the circle metaphor has value as well.

In our story we have dear Dorothy, fully in survival mode, in a house that appears in this altered state to be lifted off its foundations by the furious wind and sent flying through the spiraling tornado. The world appears to be passing by outside the window at breakneck speed. At first, ordinary farm folk fly by doing everyday things—an old lady sits in a rocking chair knitting, and a cow stands mooing placidly in the eye of the storm. A couple of fellows row a boat through the twisting storm. Suddenly Miss Gulch appears pedaling furiously on her bicycle and scowling—the very image of evil itself. As Dorothy's consciousness deepens, the woman transforms into a witch dressed in black, flying on her broom and cackling wildly against the wind.

The witch is the first archetypal character that Dorothy meets in her dream. As the Ozian counterpart of Miss Gulch, the witch is the most negative figure in the dream. She is the shadow of Dorothy. Remember that Dorothy has great feelings of hostility, too. When Miss Gulch comes to take away her dog, Dorothy advances on her in a threatening manner and says, "Ooh, I'll bite you myself, you wicked old witch."

It may be that Dorothy resents the helplessness of her auntie and uncle, the dreariness and stuckness of her surroundings. Dorothy may also have unresolved resentment toward Auntie Em, who instructed her to give her dog to Miss Gulch.

The witch is the shadowed projection of Dorothy's own resentment and hostility taken to its ultimate form. In all great initiatory experience, a person meets the shadow or evil within and must understand and conquer it before one can return home again. Think for a moment about the people you dislike the most. Might they be holding some quality of yours that you dread, but they are playing out in a big way as a mirror for you? We project our shadows onto others so that we don't have to deal with them ourselves.

The shadow is something we generally try to ignore in our body-mind system, but we need to remember that shadows activate our story. The bleakness of Kansas is a tremendous shadow that prods Dorothy to make a change. Without this prodding, there would be no story. What shadows are currently moving you? Pressing you to make a shift or at least getting you to take a look at something you may not wish to look at? I urge you to be bold! In the mythic journey, we can recognize these things and take steps to reflect upon and resolve some of the issues they bring up.

When the house reaches the top of the cyclone, it is thrown from the vortex and begins to fall from the sky. Dorothy spins around and around in her bed, screaming. The house lands with a sudden, jarring *thump!* and all is still. Having survived the crash, Dorothy rises from the bed and opens the door to the outer world to find something utterly unexpected.

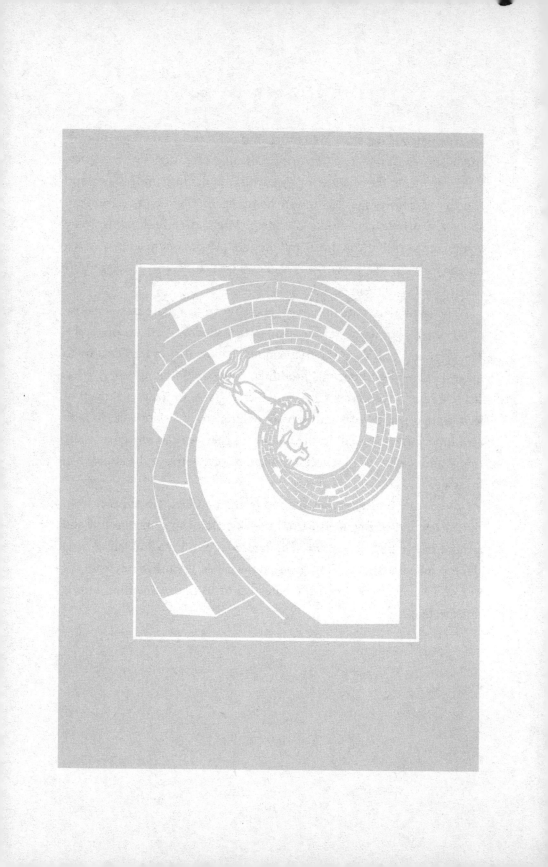

3

FOLLOW THE YELLOW
BRICK ROAD

Wonders meet Dorothy's eyes as she opens the door and is greeted by a world flooded with Technicolor. Where Kansas was a monotonous gray, she now finds herself in a landscape draped with vibrant flowers and plants of many shapes and sizes growing throughout a seemingly peaceful small village. Dorothy has also become colorful with her bright gingham dress and rosy cheeks. Behind her there is mysterious laughter and tittering amid the birdsong. She leans over to the little dog in her arms and says softly, "Toto, I have a feeling we're not in Kansas anymore."

A luminous bubble appears in the distance and glides toward Dorothy, growing larger as it approaches. It settles at the girl's feet and dissolves to reveal the cosmic supernatural source of this extended, verdant land in the radiant form of Glinda, the Good Witch of the North. Serene, calm, and confident, Glinda embodies the archetype of the benign protector, a figure who appears in all myths and lives within everyone. Glinda may also be seen as Dorothy herself—the girl's entelechy—writ large on the stage of consciousness.

Entelechy is a Greek word that means "the fullest realized essence of a thing." For example, a grand oak tree is the entelechy of an acorn; a full-grown adult is the entelechy of a human infant. If we look at ourselves mythically, the entelechy would be the part of ourselves that has had thousands of years to expand, learn, and evolve. It is the fullest realized aspect of our selves. And though we all carry this entelechy within ourselves, the Essential Self is often externalized as a separate character in myths and fairy tales to make the story more interesting to follow than a contemplative hero sitting under a tree quietly meditating on her rich inner life. In Oz, Glinda serves in this powerful, spiritual role for Dorothy.

On her throat Glinda wears a necklace adorned with a beautiful butterfly—symbol of the soul in many cultures. She is the all-seeing, all-knowing connection to Source. Think of your entelechy as your best friend and ally. As we go along in the story, we see that Glinda, like a best friend, watches over Dorothy with tremendous love and interest every step of the way, though her presence is invisible to the girl throughout most of the adventure. She is the gentle guide who allows Dorothy to learn and become stronger through her trials. She does not interfere with the process of Dorothy discovering who she really is through both the adversity and the good experiences she has with her new friends in Oz; however, when things seem hopeless for the girl and the allies cry out for help, Glinda sends help or shows up in person.

Know that the part of you that is your entelechy and all of those energies of the archetypal realm recognize and yearn to work with you as much or even more than you yearn to work with them. They grow to know themselves through us as we experience life; your entelechy is eager to build a closer relationship with you.

Process: Meeting Your Entelechy

To experience this connection, take a moment now to stand comfortably straight with your weight balanced equally on both feet. Close your eyes. Take three deep breaths in through your nose and out through your mouth. Breathe all the way down into your belly. With each breath, feel your body relaxing.

Imagine that you, like Dorothy, find yourself in a beautiful place. From the sky you notice a giant shimmering bubble floating down toward the very spot where you are standing. The bubble gets bigger and bigger as it approaches until it finally dissolves completely, revealing a glorious being of light standing directly in front of you. It is your entelechy—the Great Friend. You greet each other warmly. Now raise both of your hands in front of you so that the palms are up, facing away from your physical body and toward the light body of your entelechy. Notice that the entelechy's hands are also raised, facing you. Your palms touch, and the entelechy begins to beam waves of love into you. You take them in. Wisdom, compassion, kindness, strength—all of these things are being poured into you now through this Great Friend. Do this for a few minutes. Receive, receive, receive.

With your physical body, now step forward into the place where the entelechy is standing and turn around, facing the spot you just left. Keep your hands raised and touch the imaginary hands of your local self with your palms. You have now become the entelechy beaming energy, love, power, gratitude, and blessings into your local self. Do this for a few minutes.

With your physical body, step forward and turn around again, returning to the spot where you originally stood, palms out, facing the Great Friend. Once again receive all the good things that the entelechy is offering you. Feel yourself being filled, revitalized, and energized with your True Essence.

You may wish to repeat these steps several more times until you feel infused with the light and energy of your Great Friend. When you have finished, thank your entelechy. Know that this being loves you and is always available for you.

When you are ready, take a few more deep breaths, return to the room, and open your eyes. Look around you. Do you notice anything different? How do you feel? Those with whom I have done this process often tell me that objects seem brighter and that they feel perfectly calm and grounded.

Dorothy connects with this Great Friend within minutes of her arrival in Oz, this part of herself that embodies all of her greatest attributes. The Good Witch of the North is a fascinating character and an archetype that was unique when *The Wizard of Oz* first appeared on movie screens. Glinda (played by Billie Burke in the film) immediately asks Dorothy, "Are you a good witch or a bad witch?" The girl states that she is not a witch at all and that witches are old and ugly. The Munchkins, who are hiding in the bushes nearby, find this statement quite amusing because, as the beautiful Glinda reveals, "You see, I *am* a witch." Thus the character shatters in one sentence the stereotype of the withered, malevolent witch so often seen in traditional European fairy tales. Dorothy's entelechy then takes the role of a powerful *good* witch in our story, a type of fairy godmother and Quantum Partner full of love and care for the little girl. (*Quantum Partners* is a term I use to describe a relationship between ourselves and our entelechies and archetypal friends. They are the parts of us that are more available to larger realities, spiritual helpfulness, even cosmic agendas. Think of them as evolutionary agents, helpers on your path to living a greater story, storied beings themselves who are service-oriented professionals in the Universe's business of making better people, better societies, better worlds. Having said this, please note that I suspect my description of Quantum Partners is true but not accurate, as opposed to accurate but not true!)

Glinda descends to greet Dorothy in this unfamiliar place right away to make sure it is the girl, rather than the Wicked Witch of the West, who gets the magical ruby slippers. She also wishes to celebrate Dorothy's choice to leave Kansas in order to take on the larger, mythical life, and she wants to set our heroine on the right path that will lead to her expanded knowing and adventure.

In Joseph Campbell's Hero's Journey, once the reluctant hero first hears and then refuses the Call to Adventure, he often receives Supernatural Aid from a guide or magical helper to enable the Crossing of the Threshold into the field of adventure itself. Certainly Glinda is this all-knowing friend who teaches Dorothy the rules of a new reality in the marvelous realm of Oz, for here the rules and limits are not yet known to her.

Like Dorothy in her first moments in Oz, we must expand quickly in order to remain balanced in the rapidly changing world in which we find ourselves. Almost every day we may feel we have new things to learn, new technologies to assimilate, new "rules." We may feel we lack certain skills that would be helpful to us along the path of our journey. Fortunately, we are not alone. Just as Dorothy has, we have inner guidance available to us at all times: our own deep wisdom taking different forms. Setting aside the time to be still and connect with our own entelechy, or True Essence, often leads to amazing insights and inspirations, even skill enhancement. Hundreds of research subjects in altered states of consciousness and many thousands of participants in my seminars describe adventures of the soul so grand, so mythic, and yet so redolent of universal themes that I can readily testify to the existence of a collective pool of myth and archetype residing in each human being as part of his or her natural equipment.

This joining of the local life to the great life is a central experience of what I call *sacred psychology*. It differs from ordinary psychology in that it provides ways of moving from outmoded existence to an amplified life that is at once more cherished and more cherishing. It requires that we undertake the extraordinary task of dying to our current, local selves and of being reborn to our eternal selves. When we descend into the forgotten knowing of earlier or deeper phases of our existence, we often find hidden potentials, the unfulfilled and unfinished seeding of what we still contain, which myth often disguises as secret or special helpers.

As the story of *The Wizard of Oz* unfolds, Dorothy acquires three helpful allies, in addition to Glinda. Toto, the energy of the life force in the form of the enthusiastic canine companion ever-faithful to Dorothy, also is considered an important ally. (It is interesting to note that the Latin *in toto* means "complete or entirely."[1])

Back in Kansas, Toto was a catalyst for change who set things in motion so the girl could begin her journey. To Dorothy, some of the events may have appeared to be shadows on the surface, but in looking at the bigger picture, they occurred for good reasons. For example, it was Toto who bit Miss Gulch, releasing a chain of events that led our young heroine to Oz. If Toto had not done that, he would not have been threatened with death and captured by Miss Gulch, only to escape and return home. Because of these events, Dorothy chose to take her dog and run away from the farm she had always known. Because she ran away, she was not at home when the tornado descended. Had she been at home, she would have been safely tucked into the root cellar with Auntie Em, Uncle Henry, and the farmhands. She would have remained stuck in an outmoded situation that no longer served her. It is Toto, the life force, who pushes the girl forward. Again and again, the little terrier seizes opportunities and acts decisively with brains, love, and great courage, the theme of the entire story. Everything is in order. Everything that happens is for Dorothy's Highest Good. She is never a victim. She is surrounded by support at every turn, though she may not realize it at times. The life force itself is definitely an ally.

Quantum Partners can take many other forms, depending on a person's specific needs. I often take students down into a private, interior place where they meet the "master teacher" of the quality or capacity they wish to acquire in their conscious life. I view these special helpers as forgotten or neglected potentials for living the larger life.

Quantum Partners are the deep codings of the Source—the Infinite as it is to be found within each of us. I lead students into enactments aimed at rediscovering skills—a capacity for art or composing music, writing, or even a sense of empathy—they once knew but lost somehow, perhaps in childhood. They may also discover skills they never knew they had. Through these connections, the old toxicities and diminishments are released; access to our inner storehouse of capacities is gained and can then be used to prepare for the greater agenda—becoming an instrument through which the Source may play its great music. Then, like the hero or heroine of myth, we may, regardless of our circumstances, become an inspiration for helping culture and consciousness move toward its next level of possibility. We begin to live out of our True Essence, which is always too large for our contracted consciousness to contain. In reality, we are all of it. Each of us holds within us every archetype, every possibility. We simply need to tap into the aspect of our inner selves that best serves us daily or in a particular situation.

Process: Entering into a Relationship with a Quantum Partner

How do you enter into a real, ongoing relationship with a Quantum Partner? First, it is important that there be a rich use of imagery in your evocation of a Quantum Partner or an archetype. In meditation or active imagination, you invite the Great Partner to join you, consciously evoking visual, auditory, tactile, olfactory, and other sensory images of the one with whom you wish to work. Allow your entelechy to reveal itself to you in its own distinctive form, or choose someone who is personal and unique to you (such as Beatrice was for Dante, as the inner teacher Philemon was to Carl Jung, or as the Greek goddess Athena is to me.) At first, images may not come at all. Do not be discouraged.

Does the archetype you are calling have a physical appearance, or is the archetype a pattern of energy or light? Whatever the image may be, play with it, and soon you will find that it plays back with you, taking on greater specificity. If, like me, you are more kinesthetic and auditory, then feel and listen for your partner. You may find yourself hearing words or music, or you may be drawn to dance.

I have found in my research that the dominant inner sense soon activates the nondominant ones, and before long you have most if not all of the previously dormant senses involved in your meditations, and the relationship with your partner is increasingly concrete. A sweep of color, a cascade of images, a symphonic play or feeling, a knowing that is as deep as it is beyond the powers of speech to express—such experiences can be the forms of outreach this Quantum Partner uses to awaken your awareness to its presence.

If you take the time to establish a connection, and a relationship is cultivated, you may find yourself guided by the archetype into a larger story, often of mythic proportions, where journeys may be taken, challenges offered, and training in the depths may be experienced. There may be initiations or places and times of making important transitions that attend the acquisition of inner learning. Gradually you may gain a far larger perspective as you move out of limited time and space into Great Time and Great Story. This knowledge places your bitterness and frustration over the injustices and evils you see around you in a broader context. The transtemporal perspective of the Archetypal World brings a sense of wisdom and discrimination to the challenges of the times. A steadfast commitment to the spiritual journey may come your way in a most remarkable fashion. It seems that you have clearly been put on a journey of transformation that provides for a deep maturation of the psyche and access to the potentials of your own being. You become a celebrant and explorer, a settler and guide for others in this new world of loving partnership.

In order to facilitate this partnership, and to sharpen the tools you use to navigate this new, possible world we are creating, I now take you through a process that activates and increases all of your sensory perceptions and stimulates your creativity. By doing your inner work through the exercises in this book, you expand your capacities and manifest things more easily in your outer world.

Process: Sharpening the Senses

Imagine entering an entirely new dimension of sight, sound, smell, and taste, as Dorothy does when she takes her first steps into Oz. She finds herself immersed in a place like no other she has ever experienced. All of her senses have to be on high alert in order for her to fully take in both the wonders and the dangers that exist over the rainbow.

Let's explore what this may be like for Dorothy. Begin this process by sitting comfortably with your feet flat on the floor. Take three easy, deep breaths in through your nose and out through your mouth. Relax your body more with each breath.

Wake up your brain to new possibilities by gently tapping all around your head. Tap your temples as we begin to speak directly to your brain, your dear friend, in order to enhance the way it perceives every sight, sound, smell, and taste that you encounter, as well as everything you touch.

Put your hands down and feel yourself breathing into your brain. Imagine that when you inhale you are breathing directly into your brain, giving it deep air. Keep breathing deeply, all the way into your brain, and then breathe out. Repeat this action several times while focusing on the brain with full, circular breaths. Do this for a minute or so.

Shift your attention from your brain to your eyes. Breathe into your eyes in the same way you did your brain. At the same time, rub your hands together briskly and place them about half an inch away from your eyes, with the fingers pointing toward your eyes so that there is a kind of acceleration of energy flowing through them. (A form of light energy does actually flow through your fingertips—it has been measured.) Imagine this light going directly into your eyes, bathing them in soothing energy that enhances your ability to envision things in your world. You can see more and see better than ever before.

Let your fingers also go toward the place we think of as the third eye in the middle of the forehead, so that your capacity for inner sight and deep seeing is also enriched. Allow the energy from your fingertips to flow, and prepare to enter Oz.

Allow your hands to rest in your lap once again while you focus with your newly expanded eyes on the left side of your brain. Breathe into the left side of the brain. Give it a little warm-up and actually move your eyes toward the left side of the brain. As you activate the visual centers, you also activate the creative and imaging centers of your brain.

Using the left side of your brain, imagine that you are opening the wooden farmhouse door and looking out at a revealed world of vibrant color. Welcome to the Land of Oz. Brimming with curiosity and excitement, you step outside and look up. The blue of the sky is beyond any blue imaginable. Your eyes take in the full brilliance of your surroundings: the deep purple and gold, the blushing pink richer in hue than any sunrise, the orange brighter than any tangerine.

Allow your eyes to bathe the right side of your brain with light and energy as you breathe into the right side of your brain and physically move your eyes in that direction. Focusing on the right side of your brain, imagine a tree in Munchkinland that is full of fruit. You have never seen fruit of this kind before; it is neither plum nor pear nor peach but something new and wondrous. A crimson bird takes a piece of fruit and flies off, its wings rotating like the rotors of a helicopter.

On the left side of your brain, you walk across a clipped chartreuse lawn to the Munchkinland town square. You observe the Munchkins' curved houses and small, white buildings with thatched or shingled roofs nestled beside a pond that reflects the brilliant blue of the sky. Surrounding the village are enormous plants with shining leaves as large as opened umbrellas, flowers as broad as dinner platters, buds as big as teacups.

On the right side of your brain, you watch Toto enthusiastically sniffing the enormous water lilies floating close to the edge of the pond. He bats at one of the flowers with his paw, creating a ripple that moves all the way across the water, bumping the other water lilies along the way.

Rub your hands together briskly once again and place them about half an inch from your ears, with your fingers of energy and light pointing inward toward your ears. Energetically cleanse and clarify your capacity to hear. Allow your hands to rest on your lap and imagine that on the left side of your brain you can hear the sounds of nature in Oz. Birds are cawing, chirping, and tweeting in a rich cacophony; some seem to be speaking a language rather than singing. The water in the emerald creek chuckles at you, the grass sighs as you step on it, and the breeze whispers secrets into your ears. Toto barks, and the birds scatter.

Move your attention to the right side of your brain, where you can hear a soft noise like a hundred tinkling bells coming from a very large bubble that is floating down toward the Munchkinland. Toto barks again. Glinda appears in a shower of light and smiles at you. Mysterious giggling comes from the bushes beside you. The Good Witch calls to the Munchkins, the little inhabitants of the village, to come out of the bushes where they have been hiding. They rustle the foliage as they emerge and then tiptoe toward you with great curiosity, for they have seen nothing like you before. The diminutive citizens dressed in dazzling attire greet you politely with bows and waves and tips of their hats.

On the left side of your brain, you hear the Munchkins begin to sing in high, clear voices to celebrate your arrival. You can pick out each amazing voice and hear them combine into pleasing harmonies. They clap their hands, cheer, and stomp their shoes on the cobble-

THE WIZARD OF US

stones. The ladies swish their dresses in time to the music as they move along.

On the right side of your brain, you suddenly hear the trumpets, horns and drums of a brass band playing a stirring march. At the same time, you hear the synchronized steps of the village's uniformed soldiers clomping into the square.

Rub your hands together briskly once more, and then place your fingers of energy and light about half an inch away from your nostrils. Pour this energy into your nose so that you may capture the many interesting fragrances of Oz.

Let your hands rest as you inhale all kinds of wondrous scents— eucalyptus, pears, and roses—on the left side of your brain. In the Munchkin bakery, a batch of piping hot cinnamon rolls has just been taken out of the oven to cool on the open windowsill. Nearby, a Munchkin family must be having dinner in one of the houses for the air is filled with the aroma of a hearty stew filled with garden vegetables and fresh herbs. You can also pick out the faint, though distinct, scent of steaming mugs of hot apple cider with ginger, as well as a fragrance so familiar to you back in Kansas—hot corn on the cob with butter and a sprinkle of black pepper. Take a moment to really inhale each scent.

On the right side of your brain, you stand overlooking vast rolling fields of poppies. The rich, green smell of spring fills your nostrils: freshly turned soil, new-mown grass, and the sweet scent of lilacs bursting into bloom.

On the left side of your brain, there is the dizzying rush of what can only be sulfur and brimstone that sticks to the back of your throat. Something loathsome has recently been menacing the Munchkins, and you find it astonishing that one smell can conduct such a pungent symphony in your nose.

A brisk breeze blows past you, carrying smells from a dark forest not too far away where the right side of your brain detects pine-scented air followed by the stink of plant decay mixed with stagnant, muddy pools. You can also detect dry leaves, the acrid memory of smoke, and an unexpected whiff of wet monkey fur.

After rubbing your hands together to build up the energy once more, open your mouth a bit and let your fingers of light activate your taste buds. When you have done that, let your hands rest in your lap and move your attention to the left side of your brain. Remember the first time you tasted a sun-kissed strawberry? One of the Munchkin children offers you a china bowl filled with ripe, freshly picked berries, and you savor each juicy bite.

Focus now on the right side of your brain, where you get to taste the gigantic lollipop handed to you by members of the Lollipop Guild. The treat is sticky and sweet, and its flavor reminds you of ice cream: vanilla bean and dark chocolate.

On the left side of your brain, you realize that you are a bit hungrier than you had thought. You reach into your basket, retrieve a few of your favorite salty multigrain crackers that you tossed in there before you left Kansas, and gobble them down.

You brush the crumbs from your clothes and move your attention to the right side of your brain, where the mayor of the Munchkin village asks if you are thirsty after your journey from the sky. He offers you a cool glass of lavender lemonade, which refreshes you.

Rub your hands together briskly once again and move them a few inches apart, facing each other. Feel the energy flowing between them. You are activating your sense of touch.

Place your hands in your lap and move your attention to the left side of your brain. You feel the light pressure and tingling of Glinda's warm hand on your back. A beautiful white and gold carriage pulled by two black ponies rolls up to you. The driver beckons for you to take a ride. One of the ponies nuzzles your hand. His nose is fuzzy, and you can feel the friendly creature's breath in your palm.

Moving to the right side of your brain, you reach down to pick up Toto and stroke his wiry fur to reassure him. He wags his tail, and you both climb into the carriage. Feel the weight and warmth of his body on your lap.

Shift your focus to the left side of your brain. You rest your hand on the silky cushions of the carriage with Toto happily watching all the action taking place around you.

Now on the right side of your brain, you get out of the carriage and step up to receive the Wicked Witch of the East's death certificate from the local coroner. He shakes your hand to congratulate you for dispatching the witch with your house, and you feel the pressure of his small, weathered palm in your own. The Munchkin hands over the official document for you to examine, and you take it, feeling the stiff, crackly parchment with your fingertips.

Now take in a deep breath and move your back a bit from side to side. Relax and breathe into your entire brain. Let all of the images that you've imagined move across, so that the left side of your brain is on the right and the right side is on the left. Take all that you have seen with your expanded vision in Oz, all that you heard with your expanded hearing, all that you have smelled and tasted and touched, and allow them to come together.

Let all that you have experienced move from your brain down into your heart. The heart also sees, hears, smells, tastes, touches, and is inspired by it all. With fully activated senses and the combined energies of heart and mind, you and Dorothy are now prepared to continue this exciting journey in this new world.

The society in which the Munchkins live is similar to an early Elizabethan society with a sheriff, coroner, judge, soldiers, various guilds and leagues, arts, and dancers decked out in bright, creative clothing. It is a far richer and more cultured society than the one Dorothy has just left. It is the high culture of the depth world.

When the Munchkins see that the Wicked Witch of the East, a malevolent being who has plagued their society, has been killed by Dorothy (accidentally), they immediately recognize the girl as the savior, a being full of magic and marvels who has freed them. The crowd cheers with great gusto, and a grand celebration spontaneously occurs. Dorothy, who had no power against Miss Gulch in Kansas, is now empowered and appreciated as a kind of goddess figure and, as we know, appreciation appreciates. For probably the first time in her life, little Dorothy is seen and known in her fullness, and because of that, she is able to take on the great journey of the soul. She has entered the Other World, where she will find the sources and experiences of her true humanity.

Think now of all the people you have helped in big or little ways. You may not even remember some of them. In fact, your contact with them may have been such that you are not aware of the remarkable impact you had on their lives. Yet they all regard you as very special, held in gratitude and honor in their own particular hall of fame. Sense them now, cherishing you. All of them, known and unknown, each giving you the empowering gift of their love and gratitude. Accept that empowering gift and allow yourself to feel cherished.

The town's merriment is disrupted by the sudden appearance of the Wicked Witch of the West, who arrives in a cloud of sulfur and smoke to claim all that remains of her deceased, crushed sister: the red ruby slippers on her feet (silver shoes in Baum's book), which jut out from under the edge of the house. The ruby slippers contain all kinds of powers that the witch hopes to abuse. She grabs for the shoes, but they are magically transferred by Glinda to Dorothy's feet. "Give me those slippers!" the Wicked Witch shrieks. "I'm the only one who knows how to use them!"

Glinda whispers into Dorothy's ear, "Keep tight inside them. They must be very powerful or she wouldn't want them." In essence, the shoes are the symbol of transporting powers that can be used for good or ill.

The ruby slippers are symbolic of your own capacities that you suspect you have but don't yet know how to use. They may be on your feet or in your hands or in your mind or within your soul. Please take a moment to say out loud or write, "I think my ruby slippers are my capacity to . . ." Once you announce these things and agree to "wear" them, even though you may not be quite sure what they are, mysterious things will begin to happen.

Glinda tells the witch to be gone "before somebody drops a house on you!" The furious witch goes reluctantly, but not before she threatens Dorothy: "I'll get you my little pretty! And your little dog, too!"

It has become very clear that the girl has made a vicious enemy in this new land and must get back to Kansas as soon as possible. Glinda informs her that because she can't go back the way she came, she must travel all the way to the Emerald City to ask the Wizard of Oz for help. The delicious irony is that no sooner has Dorothy left dreary Kansas and traveled over the rainbow than she becomes desperate to return again. This tells me that we have to educate ourselves to be able to live in the extended reality of the kingdom. This is not easy. If one has lived on the outskirts for too long, the bliss tolerance may have diminished and may have to be built up again in order to live in the kingdom for any period of time. If a person is able to build it up once more, then when the return home occurs, the kingdom can be found there as well.

How long can you sustain being happy, being in a state of delight, having long pleasures and short pains rather than long pains and short pleasures? How long can you see people as allies and those around you as God in hiding? How long can you see miracles in everyday existence? How long can you live in the kingdom? Try living in the kingdom, the green land, the possible society a little longer each day.

Dorothy sets out on her journey to the Great Unknown Source—the all-powerful and very mysterious Wizard in the Emerald City, who may give her what she needs. Dorothy is also driven to return home as soon as possible because she fears that her Auntie Em has become ill, sick with worry over her missing niece, possibly even dying of a broken heart. It will be a long journey to the Emerald City and Dorothy and Toto will have to walk. "But how do I get there?" the girl asks.

Glinda advises her that it is always best to "start at the beginning." The Good Witch gestures to the tip of the spiraling Yellow Brick Road, the golden path of pilgrimage, located in the center of town. The Yellow Brick Road is similar to the walkabout of the Aborigines across great reaches of Australia. They follow the song lines of their clan, with its memories of all the places traveled by the ancestor creators. It is like the ancient Greek path traveled by the initiates of the Eleusinian Mysteries that led from Athens to the mouth of the underworld at Eleusis and back to the airy height of the Acropolis. It is the path that pilgrims would take to Compostela or to Jerusalem or to Mecca. It is the road of golden pollen set down by Spider Woman of the Navaho story so that two holy children may find their father, the Sun. It is the path that appears in all great myths.

Glinda kisses Dorothy on the forehead (the place of her third eye, her intuitive eye) before disappearing in her bubble of light, and the girl takes the first steps of her journey. The Munchkins echo Glinda's advice, enthusiastically singing and chanting, "Follow the Yellow Brick Road!" as they escort her as far as the edge of the town. With her plucky little terrier at her side, the optimistic girl waves good-bye before turning her full attention to the road ahead—the path of discovery and transformation that will take Dorothy to all parts of herself.

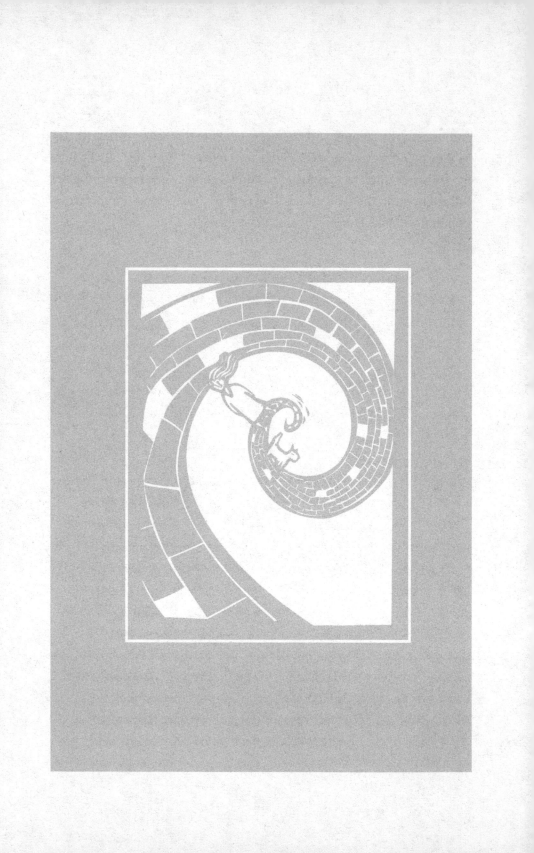

4

IF I ONLY HAD A BRAIN

Dorothy travels along the Yellow Brick Road, infused with God stuff, filled with possibilities, magical ruby slippers on her feet and the ever-enthusiastic Toto at her side. She comes to a crossroad where she pauses, having no idea which way to go. In a nearby cornfield, a funny-looking Scarecrow (played in the film by the seemingly boneless Ray Bolger) hears Dorothy wondering aloud about her direction. The Scarecrow comes to life and promptly offers her options, first pointing down one road, saying, "That's a good way," and then pointing down the other road, saying that road works just as well. Finally, he crosses his arms across his chest and points in both directions at once. Clearly, on one level, he can't make up his mind. On another level, the Scarecrow exhibits the gift of second sight and the ability to exist cheerfully in the midst of opposition.

The fork in the road is traditionally a big moment in any mythic journey because it indicates the need to see both, if not all, paths available to a life and a society. In the Hero's Journey, this critical choice point represents the separation of the hero's known world and self. It is the point in which the hero transitions between worlds and selves to see the potential for a new world and a new self. The fork in the road can be frightening—for the hero doesn't know what lies ahead—but by choosing which way on the path she will go, Dorothy also enters the stage that shows an open willingness to undergo major life change and personal transformation.

Development of the other sides of our selves in ways that allow us to be aware of them and to hold them within us simultaneously helps us navigate through a society as complex as our own in these modern times. Think of a path not taken in your life. If you had taken that "other" path, where would you be now? What would you be doing? More important, who would you be? In the Road of Trials, all roads are the right ones, even the frustrating ones, because they lead to awareness and growth of the self. If you made what you now consider to be a "wrong" turn, think of the ways that you really could have messed up on the "right" one. All roads fork. And down the path they fork again and again. Chances are your soul will lead you to the same place ultimately, regardless of which path you take. Just think about that: the fork in the road, the road not taken. What did you choose?

Process: The Roads Not Taken

As an experiment, you can write down the story of your own fork in the road, that place where you had to make a choice that changed the course of your life. Another way of doing this exercise is to draw three plausible roads from some point in your life: the road you are currently taking and the two roads you did not take. Also, draw in a picture of where you want to arrive. In good comic-strip fashion, draw or write down how you would get to your goal from where you are now, given your chosen road. Imagine the life you would have, the events that would occur. Now do the same for the other two. Voila! All three arrive at the desired destination, and you have had fun playing with parallel lives.

Observing his confusing directions, Dorothy asks the Scarecrow whether he can't make up his mind. Alas, the fellow replies, he truly can't "make up his mind" because he has no brain; his head is stuffed with nothing but straw. The girl finds this quite strange and points out the fact that he can talk and therefore must have a brain. To which the Scarecrow wittily reminds her that, "Sometimes people without brains do an awful lot of talking."

The Scarecrow worries that he's not very good at his job; the crows fly into his field only to laugh at him while they steal his corn. He feels truly stuck. But he recognizes his stuckness. And from that awareness comes the first of his brilliant inspirations: he can ask for help! He suggests to Dorothy that she turn the wooden peg that holds him upright on the pole. Maybe that action will release him. The idea works, and the fellow drops to the ground. He rises on wobbly legs and in the song lyrics by E. Y. Harburg, sings wistfully about all of the things he would do if he "only had a brain."[1]

How often do we echo that sentiment, thinking that we are not smart enough, bright enough, or even quick enough to deal with the ordeals of everyday life? It is the desire to learn, as the Scarecrow suggests, that is the key to filling up our brain maps. Otherwise we languish and lament what we see as our inadequate equipment.

Inadequate? How can we believe our brains inadequate? Within this "three-pound universe," this biomass extravaganza, is encoded the wisdom of the millennia and the dream of tomorrow, the capacity to decode even the most multifaceted symbols, and the desire for communion and community. Language, memory, and the great achievements of civilization emerge from the delicate, complex interaction of perhaps 100 billion neurons in trillions of connections Ah, "if I only had a brain."

What the Scarecrow requires, and what is accomplished as the story unfolds, is something more, a transformation of awareness about the brain and about life.

For the Scarecrow, or any of us, transformation of consciousness requires more than just a change of attitude. By looking at my own mind-research projects, as well as those of many other students of the phenomenon, I believe we can say with confidence that a genuine transformation of consciousness engenders structural and chemical changes in the brain that affect those who experience them both psychologically and physiologically. I also believe that this internal transformation affects the energy field in which we live, thus changing the world around us. My studies have been primarily in the areas of creativity and altered states, but there is extraordinary work being done on the study of the brain, called neuroplasticity.

A wonderful exploration of this field is found in the book *The Brain that Changes Itself* by Norman Doidge. The brain is not hardwired, as we all thought; it is not a complex machine that cannot change. On the contrary, the brain has remarkable capacities for reorganizing and regrowing itself so that if one part fails, another part that seemingly has little to do with that particular function can take over; if there is a death of brain cells, there is also a concomitant rebirth of new ones. Brain circuits can recircuit themselves.[2]

Innovative scientists such as Bruce Lipton are showing that thinking, learning, acting, intending, meditating, and enjoying experiences can activate the basic genetic structures of our bodies, brains, and minds so that we can literally shape our brain anatomy and behavior, and we can grow new capacities and even a newly evolved human version of ourselves. The term *neuroplasticity* is derived from *neuro*, the nerve cells in our brains and nervous systems, and *plasticity*, for the changeable, malleable, modifiable aspect of the brain.

In other words, you have a brain whose architecture is changing all the time. How you work with your brain—give it nourishment, ideas, therapy, along with spiritual, mental, and emotional practices and input—radically influences what your brain can and will be. The effect of culture, music, relationships of all kinds, intimacy, learning, grief, addiction, technology, the internet, and even seminars affect this brain of yours and consequently affect what you are able to do with it, which, simply put, is quite a lot!

In the distant past, when we depended on our brain for survival in challenging weather, like the ice ages, or very difficult circumstances, like finding food and shelter and avoiding being killed by four-legged or two-legged beings, we routed our brains along certain growth patterns that grew our brains with regard to certain kinds of intelligences and skills and adaptations that kept us alive. Today's challenges are as great if not greater, given that we are faced with world-destroying possibilities and the archaic reactions to them that, it would seem, were cooked up in ancient caves. Clearly, if we are going to survive and champion a time of transformation, we need to do something remarkable with our own brains.

Research into other realities of the brain has been no less amazing. Mirror neurons are my particular favorites of these mind-blowing discoveries. For example, suppose you learn to play a sequence of notes on the piano; as you do that, your brain's electric activity in specific areas is changing and can be observed on the wondrous machinery capable of mapping such action. Now, when you simply watch someone play that tune, or even when you simply sit in front of a piano and just think about playing the same notes, the same changes are occurring in your brain. It is the virtual made real, a solid quantification of the power of thought. I have often seen similar demonstrations of mind-brain wonders in my work with time distortion and subjective realities.

I am entranced by these studies of our electrochemical brains, yet for *The Wizard of Us*, I am inviting us to engage philosophical and psychological structures that may not be capable of being mapped physically. At least, not yet. Just because the spirit cannot be measured nor the soul charted does not mean that they do not exist or that they do not have profound powers to influence the mind and being of a person. For we know that neuroplasticity may prove to be a curse as well. The brain can think itself into ruts, with electrical habits as difficult to eradicate as if it were, in fact, the immutable machine of yore. And, of course, the implications for external reengineering of the human brain are ominous, for if the brain is malleable, it is also endlessly vulnerable, not only to its own mistakes but also to the ambitions and excesses of others, whether they are misguided parents, well-meaning cultural trendsetters, or despotic national leaders.

The new science of the brain may still be in its infancy, but already, as Doidge made quite clear, the scientific minds are leaping ahead. Doidge described Michael Merzenich, a leading researcher in neuroplasticity:

Merzenich's specialty is improving people's ability to think and perceive by redesigning the brain by training specific processing areas, called brain maps, so that they do more mental work. He has also, perhaps more than any other scientist, shown in rich scientific detail *how* our brain-processing areas change. . . . That brain exercises may be as useful as drugs to treat diseases as severe as schizophrenia; that plasticity exists from the cradle to the grave; and that radical improvements in cognitive functioning—how we learn, think, perceive, and remember—are possible even in the elderly. . . . Merzenich argues that practicing a new skill, under the right conditions, can change hundreds of millions and possibly billions of the connections between the nerve cells in our brain maps.[3]

Doidge continued by explaining Merzenich's concepts of how the brain learns:

Merzenich claims that when learning occurs in a way consistent with the laws that govern brain plasticity, the mental "machinery" of the brain can be improved so that we learn and perceive with greater precision, speed, and retention.

Clearly when we learn, we increase what we know. But Merzenich's claim is that we can also change the very structure of the brain itself and increase its capacity to learn. Unlike a computer, the brain is constantly adapting itself.

"The cerebral cortex," he says of the thin outer layer of the brain, "is actually selectively refining its processing capacities to fit each task at hand." It doesn't simply learn; it is always "learning how to learn." The brain Merzenich describes is not an inanimate vessel that we fill; rather it is more like a living creature with an appetite, one that can grow and change itself with proper nourishment and exercise.[4]

Why do children up to about the age of thirteen learn languages so quickly? In part, it is because they have not filled out their linguistic brain map with their native tongue. Thus, a child can simultaneously learn French and English and Chinese because they still have the space on their linguistic brain map to do so. Later in life we have filled up large parts of that map with our primary language, so we are always pushing and squeezing the brain map to learn the other language. My own experiments, however, show that if I add gestures, visualizations, feelings, and moods to the language learning, then people can pick up the language they want to learn much faster because they are giving the language patterns over to another part of the brain.

I have always been fascinated by the question of what we might achieve if we had the same kind of neuroplasticity that we had as children, when we learned so much in such a short time. Some of my work over many years designing brain exercises and, with the coming of computer programs, the work of scientists like Merzenich to create programs that train the mind to focus, to pick up speed, to recognize patterns seem to have the effect of staving off mental deterioration as we age and reactivating some of the potential for learning languages and skills that we had as children. As children we are always learning new things as well as acquiring new skills and their applications.

Merzenich believes "our neglect of intensive learning as we age leads the systems in the brain that modulate, regulate, and control plasticity to waste away."[5] Anything that requires highly focused attention helps our brains not to atrophy but to continue to grow and, I believe, to grow in all kinds of new directions that were not there for us even as children. For, as adults, we have eros and aesthetic joy and a sense of the tragic things that give irony and reflection and make the sunnier things stand out in sharper contrast. We have philosophy and spiritual reflections. So when we join these experiences to learning new physical activities requiring concentration and both fine and large motor control (such as solving challenging puzzles, learning a new language, or making a career change that requires us to master new skills), we gradually sharpen our brains. It is also very important to keep our bodies' motor skills up—whether by dancing or engaging in a sport, as these sorts of activities allow the motor parts of the brain to affect acuity, focus, and speed in the more conceptual areas.

Guess who demonstrates these enchanting truths about the ever-changing, ever-growing brain? None other than our old friend the Scarecrow. He's a true teacher of how to grow a brain. First, he engages with another creature. Into his field come Dorothy and her red shoes, with the vibrant explorer Toto. She grants him the opportunity to engage by asking questions. Right away all three of their brains are changing.

Then the Scarecrow acknowledges his condition as stuck. And that he feels like a failure. Next he imagines that his condition might be helped (he might be able to create a brain) if he asks for assistance. Two things have happened: he has imagined a new possibility for himself, and he has seen the first necessary step, get unstuck! No matter what.

Notice that he falls into a heap at first, allowing his new brain the time required to become adjusted to the fact that everything is changing. In honor of that moment of quiescence (and perhaps all that time he spent being a Scarecrow, looking at the sun and moon and all the world around him), let us turn for a moment to the field of study known as contemplative neuroscience. The word *contemplative* refers to a quiet interlude, allowing a person to focus on inner realities.

During this interlude our Scarecrow's changing brain finds its most potent power, that of the imagination. He then draws himself up and initiates the next potent practice to awaken the brain: movement. He dances, he cavorts, and he sings out his dreams—all of them having to do with inner growth and contemplation—of whiling away the hours, talking to flowers, inventing and solving riddles, and thinking things no one has ever thought before.

As we begin to engage the process of growing our brain at ever-deepening levels, we first renew our commitment to cultivating our inner lives. Here we use the resources of spiritual technology to turn inward to meet and receive reality in its fullness. Our current historical epoch is unique in that the spiritual technologies at our disposal can be harvested from the whole world: Christian centering prayer, Native American ritual and shamanic practices, Jungian dreamwork, meditation as practiced in the Hindu religion, as well as Buddhist mindfulness and visualization. Whatever discipline is chosen, work and focus are required to make it a continuous factor in our lives. Many people today actively avail themselves of the richness now at hand to organize for themselves a menu of practices that speaks to their particular needs and preferences. All involve reworking the landscapes of the subliminal mind so that there are channels and riverbeds in which deeper spiritual consciousness can flow. The latest science suggests that the *physical* brain is actually positively altered as a result of deep meditation and contemplation.

Neuropsychologist Rick Hanson wrote a revealing book, *Buddha's Brain* with neurologist Richard Mendius. In it, Hanson discussed the physical and measurable effect meditation has on the human brain.[6] Hanson, who is also a meditation teacher, said that we do not need to frame a contemplative practice with reference to God to get good results in the brain: "Although the word contemplative sounds fancy looking up at the stars, going to the ocean and getting a sense of the enormity of it all, or looking into your baby's eyes and thinking *Holy Moly, how did I get you and how did you get me?* All of that is contemplative."[7] Scarecrow practices contemplation playfully and plans not only to study the ocean but also to discover and reveal some of its secrets—"why the ocean's near the shore," for example.[8]

Hanson explained that twice as much is known about the brain today as was known in 1990 and a hundred times more is known about the effect of contemplative neuroscience than was known at that time. Neuroscientists now have proof through medical MRIs that the brain actually becomes built up in people who have regular meditation or a contemplative practice. Synapses are built, and people are able to focus their attention better. The insula becomes thicker, which helps a person to become more aware and empathetic because the insula is responsible for tracking "the interior state of the body and the feelings of other people."[9]

Canadian psychologist Donald Hebb explained that "neurons that fire together wire together."[10] Hanson shared how this works in simple terms:

> The mind takes the shape of whatever it rests upon—or more exactly, the brain takes the shape of whatever the mind rests upon. So, if you regularly rest your mind on regrets, resentments, quarrels with others, self-reproach—you know, the voice in the back of your head yammering away about what a nobody you really are and if others only knew you better, etcetera—if you rest your mind there, it will change your brain in that direction, because neurons that fire together wire together, for better or worse.[11]

This means that we could absolutely engage in self-directed neuroplasticity by taking time out of each day to consciously replace the negative tapes that we may have been playing with thoughts of happiness, love, and wisdom.

Again the Scarecrow declares he expects to do just that, once the Wizard makes it possible.

Hanson said that it is human nature to have very active "monkey minds" (literally) because in the earliest days of the evolving species, we were surrounded by danger on all sides. Humans who were not alertly using all of their senses to scan the landscape constantly for signs of possible trouble were usually eaten. We lived in fear. In our modern times, negative images and messages bombard us through the media every day, and even though it may not be our intention to do so, we take in quite a bit of it. We are so bombarded with images of things we should fear that that way of thinking becomes a habit in our brains. To shift these habits, we need to build new circuitry.[12]

Once we make ourselves truly at home in the deeper dimensions of contemplation and the imagination, we once again embark on the Yellow Brick Road and further adventures. It is the contemplation and anticipation of our visit to the Wizard that impels us—with Dorothy, Toto, and our splendidly brainy friend, the Scarecrow—to sing out our dreams and begin to live into them.

Process: Relaxing the Brain

Let's begin with a simple process. Imagining yourself having been released from your stuck place, you find yourself in a place of quiet. Perhaps, like the Scarecrow, you are aware that everything is changing now, and you want to take the time to feel your way into that new reality. Find a comfortable sitting position, close your eyes, and follow your breathing. Rest your hands in your lap and your feet flat on the floor. Inhale easily and deeply through your nose, and exhale through your mouth. Begin to relax any areas of tension in your body: shoulders, back, face—even your tongue. As you sit in stillness, in a state of peaceful equanimity, find yourself riding the waves of your own breathing. Without making an effort to do so, fill your mind, heart, and energy field with good feelings. Do this by focusing your attention on whatever causes you to feel that way. Perhaps imitate the Scarecrow: confer with flowers and consult the rain; let it feel pleasurable. Begin to experience some of the peace he feels at this possibility of contentment, even joy. This releases a steady flow of "dopamine, a neurotransmitter that tracks rewards" in the physical brain that will then "steady the mind."[13]

As you flow into deeper relaxation, picture your mind as a clear, blue sky. As thoughts arise, imagine them to be clouds that float across the sky of your consciousness. Watch them go, but do not become attached to them or follow them. As they pass away, return once more to a gentle focus on the clarity and purity of the blue, cloudless sky. Gradually, your consciousness will be only blue sky and, after that, pure consciousness with no object but itself.

Now allow yourself to imagine what you could do, "if you only had a brain." Let some of those thoughts begin to color the blue sky of your mind with gold or crimson or flowers. Focus on those dreams and ideas—new thoughts, perhaps. See them play out almost like Ray Bolger dancing down the Yellow Brick Road, toward the realm of infinite possibility. Gradually bring attention back to your breath and to yourself sitting there in the chair, having practiced contemplation.

As you continue to practice this simple meditation, the circuits in your brain recognize the routine and fire easily; the mind and body calm. With just a few minutes of practice each day, the stresses of life gradually cease to overwhelm you. Peace of mind and clarity of spirit become a way of being, as your consciousness and the Mind that is the essence of all reality come closer together, even into oneness.

In its early practice, this form of contemplation tends to require some of the same effort as learning to read—that is, a conscious changing of focus. Just as to a child the strange and baffling markings on the page gradually become letters, words, sentences, and then meaning, so to, in inward-turning contemplation, we discover a whole new way of apprehending reality that is first glimpsed, then understood, and finally grasped.

What is "read" in contemplative practice, however, is ultimately nothing short of the Absolute itself. As we move from our conditioned existence in the world of becoming to the ground of our existence in the world of being, perceptual assumptions built up by self, need, history, and everyday life dissolve. Eventually our lenses become so gossamer as to disappear. The Buddhists call the goal of such contemplation "void-ness," or *shunyata*; Christian mystics call it "emptying," or *kenosis*. Face to face with the substance of all being, the energy of creation, we discover to our deep joy that the Absolute has been our essential nature all the time, regardless of how far or how weirdly we have sought it outside of ourselves.

My good friend Deepak Chopra and I regularly give workshops together on Summoning the Sacred. During one of these gatherings, he said, "We are an infinite consciousness localized in a human brain, so we should never underestimate our power."[14] This sentiment agrees with my own feeling that the Selfing Game is what Infinity does for fun. Of course you are an evolutionary agent! Of course you are an infinite consciousness localized in a human brain with untold powers and capacities. Taking these statements into account, let us see where our speculations lead us.

In a letter to Michael Besso, Albert Einstein wrote, "I think that only daring speculation can lead us further and not accumulation of facts."[15] And so we dare to speculate on the nature of the brain in its relationship to the universe and the act of creation itself. Dare I go so far as to suggest that what you read in your contemplative journeys toward the universe will be true but not accurate, as opposed to being accurate but not true?

To begin, you discover everything is connection. Everything is connectivity, bridging, and fractal resonance. Fractals are those patterns of repetition that are similar in all levels of magnification. For instance, you look at a huge coastline and see a certain wave pattern. But look closely at the wave eddies in the sand and you see that they refract an identical coastline in miniature. The two are similar in process, if not exactly in form. Natural objects that are approximated by fractals to a degree include clouds, mountain ranges, lightning bolts, and snowflakes. Looking at trees, we see fractals of the brain and the circulatory system. Seashells are fractally related to the whorl pattern in flowers, to the ear, to the heart, to the DNA spiral. And everything is patterned after the universe to which it is connected.

Take creativity, for example. The universe is an infinitely creative organism, which imparts its creativity to us. We, in turn, reflect this by delivering our creative Nature and process to those objects of our creation. These, in turn, change the Nature of the Universe, which sparks it to still greater creativity. We are fractally together: the universe, you, and me.

It follows that, in decoding the Universe, we decode the brain; in decoding the brain, we decode the Universe. The line in Genesis about God creating human beings in His or Her image and likeness is coming to be seen as quite accurate when we enter into some of the new understandings of the brain and universe. We discover that they are alike in process, if not in form. So we might extend Genesis to read, *God created man/woman in his own fractal process, image, and likeness.* What I like to call the magnificent human is really God stuff incarnate, able to access the universal reality of which we are fractally a part. When you know yourself as the universe in innovative process, you gain a larger sense of your unique role and destiny in time.

I believe that we are a body of knowing. We only appear to be separate from the infinite universe, but the new physics show that beneath this seeming separateness, there is a deeper unity, a nonlocal connectivity to our universe. We live in a holographic universe where all is connected with all. In fact, in my years as a student of spiritual traditions and psychologies, I have found in virtually every tradition, especially in the mystical forms of each, that when we enter into the deepest parts of ourselves, we always find that we are connecting to the flow that sustains the entire universe. Therefore, we have access to the wisdom, skill, and transformative power that the universe contains. The wisdom of creation is directly accessible to us in our everyday life experience. We do not just dwell in the Universe—the Universe dwells inside us.

Jesus declared that the kingdom of God is within us, and if we look within, we discover immense wisdom within our direct experience. The kingdom is also all around us. In the Gnostic Gospel of Thomas, saying 113, Jesus is reported to have said, ". . . the Father's kingdom is spread out upon the earth, and people don't see it."[16]

So, the treasures of this kingdom are both within—the felt wisdom and the love of the heart—and without, and knowing the Universe as presence, or God's presence, infuses creation. These two, love and wisdom, are always together; in fact, they may be the same thing.

In his book *The Living Universe*, Duane Elgin said that all the world's wisdom traditions declare that this world is infused with sacred meaning and knowledge of the particular and the general, of the local and of the cosmos itself. Because we are integral to the Universe, by going into our direct experience of being alive, we have absolute knowing of everything beyond our local knowledge, reason, or even local experience:

> There is no more elevated task than to learn, of our own free will, the skills of living in eternity. In consciously becoming intimate friends with ourselves, we are directly participating in the life-stream of the universe and consciously cultivating the body of knowing that is our vehicle through the deep ecology of the Mother Universe—through eternity.[17]

Just as Dorothy's magical allies on her Hero's Journey represent the brain, the heart, and the guts to persevere for all of us, we are each here with a simple job to do—to become great and deeply committed friends to both our finite and our infinite selves, our archetypal infinite selves, enjoying the phenomenal gifts of our incarnation. Think of yourself as a flow-through of life energy. We are the closing of a cosmic loop that has been broken by living out of a limited sense of ourselves and of our reality. Now we are guided to make friends with our larger self, with our stupendous higher destiny, and in so doing, we deepen our access to intuitive wisdom, celebrating our unique gifts and realizing that we always have within us the great powers of the brain and the heart and the courage to step into our greater reality. The power to reside in our Universal home has always been within us.

It is here that you, as the artful re-creator of the self, get in touch with the healing and transforming powers and capacities within yourself. Herein, you discover the emerging patterns for your higher life as well as the emerging picture of the world that is trying to be, and also what you can do to help its becoming. The ultimate service of human life is a kind of vitality that comes out of a true sense of belonging. The Universe is holding its breath, waiting for you to take your place, no matter how humble that may be, or how small that place may be. There is no other part of creation that can substitute for you belonging to the world.

I believe that this is why the mythic story of *The Wizard of Oz* is more important now than at any time in human history. We humans are now being called to participate in our own Hero's Journey in order to experience a vastly bigger life. Otherwise, there is a strong possibility that our species will not survive. We are called to cosmic connections, to be the cosmic beings in a living Universe that we actually are, and it is time to take that call. To grow in our thinking and living into the actual scope of our being represents an extraordinary journey of awakening. It is our journey home.

So it is that Dorothy kindly invites the Scarecrow to join her on her adventure on the road to the Emerald City, explaining that the great and powerful Wizard who lives there might give him a brain. The man of straw is thrilled at the prospect, and the two friends gallop off happily down the Yellow Brick Road, singing cheerfully, with Toto trotting faithfully at their heels. During the course of this journey, the Scarecrow proves to be a genius at figuring things out. Often the very quality we think we lack is really our most potent potential. It's just been sitting up there on a pole waiting for us to notice it.

5

THE HEART OF
THE MATTER

As Dorothy and the Scarecrow travel along the Yellow Brick Road, they come upon a grove of enormous, gnarled apple trees. Dorothy is hungry and decides to pluck an apple from the closest tree, whereupon the tree slaps her hand and gruffly scolds her. In stunned surprise she cries out, "I keep forgetting I'm not in Kansas anymore."

The Scarecrow quickly assesses the situation and gets an idea. He makes a face at the trees and comments that the apples probably weren't very good anyway. His trick works and the insulted apple trees begin to pick the apples off themselves and hurl them at the man of straw and Dorothy.

While gathering apples off the ground, Dorothy makes her way up a hill, only to be confronted with a strange and unexpected sight—a man made entirely out of tin (played with great aplomb by Jack Haley, who said in an interview that he based the character's wide-eyed innocence

69

on his son, who was five years old at the time of filming). The man stands rigid and stiff, completely immobile, his axe held high. The mysterious man seems to be more than just tin and Dorothy taps on his chest as if knocking on a door to see if anyone is home. The knock is answered by a lonely echo before a tight, squeaky voice responds, "Oil can." Sure enough, an old oil can rests on a nearby stump and once Dorothy oils the Tin Man's mouth and then the rest of his joints, he is able to tell his mournful tale about the tinsmith who built him. He reveals that his innards are hollow because the man forgot to give him a heart. Then, while he, the Tin Man, was chopping a tree one day, a sudden rain shower came along and rusted him solid.

Once freed from his rusty state, the Tin Man begins to dance around and sing about what he would do if he "only had a heart."[1]

Sadly, this seems to be the story of many people who have been rusted into immobility. The Tin Man may represent the mechanization of our reality of which the loss of heart is the worst to bear. It is easy enough to get oiled and get moving, but without heart there is no impetus to keep on going. In her book *The Real Wizard of Oz*, Rebecca Loncraine wondered if Baum might have been making a statement about the increasing mechanization of society and its effect on living, breathing organisms through his character of the Tin Man, the man with no heart. She wrote:

> Machines of all kinds were entering life in 1900 and doing jobs previously performed by humans and animals. Baum's story suggests that this might have consequences; riding to work on an electric streetcar was very different than being pulled along in a horse-drawn cart, with the horse's blood pumping through its veins. Talking to someone over the telephone was very different from speaking to them face-to-face.[2]

This is an issue for us now more than ever with computers and automation taking over jobs previously performed by human beings. Texting, tweeting, and posting Facebook entries are now the common forms of communication. It is easy to feel overwhelmed by the lightning-speed technological advancement of our culture. It seems as if the smart phone we just purchased on Friday has become obsolete by Monday. As technology takes over, we might ask ourselves if we can maintain our heart connections without tipping into a feeling that we are racing on a rat wheel to keep up with it all. It is essential that we, as creators of the new world, learn to balance our technological advancements with our humanity. We must keep our hearts and minds open to give and receive if we are to become the kind of human beings our planet requires at this time in history.

Let us take a closer look at the heart. Neurons are not just located in the brain in your head, which is why ancient and indigenous civilizations place the mind in the heart region as well as in other parts of the body. The Ancient Greeks, Mesopotamians, and Babylonians spoke of the heart as the center of intelligence with its own reason and knowing. Science has shown that the heart communicates with the body and brain on various different levels. For instance, the heart sends neurological information to the brain and the rest of the body. Through the pulse, the heart sends energy in the form of a blood pressure wave, which causes changes in electrical activity in the brain. The heart communicates on a biochemical level, releasing atrial peptide, a hormone that inhibits the release of stress hormones. And the heart communicates electromagnetically: an EKG measures the electrical signals produced by the heart.

In their book *Heart-Centered Leadership*, Susan Steinbrecher and Joel B. Bennett wrote that the heart has a memory of its own. This was revealed in story after story of heart transplant recipients who suddenly displayed "psychological changes that paralleled the experiences of their donors. Parallels included preferences related to food, music, art, sex, recreation and careers, as well as specific instances of perceptions of names and sensory experiences related to donors."[3] Steinbrecher and Bennett noted that when asked about the location of the "self," people pointed to the heart area of their chests as the "seat of the soul" more often than any other place, adding that "when we fall in love, it would be ridiculous to say 'I give you my brain,' but romantic and appropriate to say 'I give you my heart.'"[4] We might say, "Let's get to the heart of the matter" when he or she means the center or core of an issue.

References to the heart and the theme of love occur throughout the writings of the world's major religions. The Old Testament alone contains over seven hundred references to the word *heart* in the New Testament there are over two hundred. The image of a heart with wings is a primary symbol of the Sufi tradition. Purity of heart seems to be a common thread in these beliefs.[5]

The Chinese believe that the heart "houses the mind," and that its health, or lack of it, affects communication, sleep, and our ability to have good emotional relationships. The heart (believed to be a feminine, or yin, organ) is related to the element of fire.[6]

The ancient Egyptians considered the heart to be the seat of the soul. When a person died, it was believed that his spirit was guided by Anubis to the Hall of Ma'at where the heart was weighed on a scale against the feather of truth. Osiris, god of the underworld, watched over the proceedings as Thoth, the ibis-headed scribe god carefully recorded the results. If the heart was found to be as light or lighter than the feather (meaning the deceased person had led a virtuous life full of good deeds while on earth), the person's spirit was allowed to move on to a happy afterlife. If the heart proved to be heavier than the feather, it meant that the person had led a wicked life and he was immediately gobbled up by the monstrous form of the god Ammut the Devourer. (Ammut was depicted as having the head of a snapping crocodile, the forequarters of a lion, and the bottom of a hippopotamus. If the thought of that waiting for you in the afterlife didn't keep you in line, what would?)

I have found that the human heart-brain, the mind, and the gut-brain provide us with an amplitude of intelligence—more than enough, in fact, to deal creatively with the challenges of changing times. Is it any wonder that Dorothy's allies down the Yellow Brick Road are searching for brains, heart, and guts, only to discover that they have these attributes in abundance? In fact, it is in dire times throughout human history and evolutionary development that all species, ourselves included, are forced to engage more of their innate intelligence, and thereby survive lest they perish. Creating a conscious partnership with these various parts of ourselves enables us to not only survive but thrive no matter what life may bring our way.

Let us stop for a moment to consider this extraordinary organ pumping inside your chest cavity. Creation of the heart is a perfect example of the physical entelechy at work. Everything in the heart is connected by electrical signals. The first fully functioning system to form in the developing human embryo is the heart and circulation. This has all occurred by the time the embryo is a mere one inch long and only eight weeks old.

The human heart beats about 100,000 times each day, and 2.5 billion times in an average lifetime. Weighing less than one pound (lighter in women than in men), it pumps blood through an intricate system of arteries, veins, and capillaries at an astounding rate of eleven pints a minute, almost 2,000 gallons a day, and over 700,000 gallons a year with strength that could shoot blood up to thirty feet. It does all of that without you having to give it a single thought.[7] Thank your heart for doing such a great job of keeping you alive.

Turn to the emotional and spiritual aspects of your heart now, particularly kindness, compassion, and empathy. How do you treat yourself? What does your inner voice sound like when you speak to yourself? Are you a severe, critical disciplinarian, putting yourself down for never doing enough? Or do you speak gently and kindly with nurturing words that uplift you and nudge you forward feeling supported? What type of thoughts are you feeding yourself?

We must fill our own internal wells before we can move out into the world to help others. One way we can open our hearts to ourselves more fully is by sitting quietly, stopping the mind chatter for a moment, and truly listening to the wisdom of our bodies. Just as we learned to pick up external cues with our heightened sensory exercise in chapter 2, now we must turn within to pick up the cues there. Ask yourself, *What does my body need in this moment? Am I giving it enough sleep or rest?* Consistently denying the body adequate sleep seems to be a common practice in many parts of the world in these modern times. In a *Guardian* news article by Peter Walker, Francesco Cuppuccio, professor at the University of Warwick and head of an international study on sleep deprivation, was quoted as saying that "modern society has seen a gradual reduction in the amount of sleep people take, suggesting that it may be due to societal pressure for working longer hours and more shift-work."[8] The results of this study, conducted over twenty years with over a million male and female participants in the United States, Asia, and Europe, found that a constant lack of sleep could contribute to a person's early death.

According to a related article entitled "Sleep Disorder Research: The Brain's Response to Lack of Sleep," our brains and bodies repair themselves while we are asleep: "Missing one or two hours of sleep for one night will not only reduce your energy level, it can decrease your brain power by one third. Lack of sleep does more damage than lack of food."[9] Not giving the body the sleep it requires affects decision-making, energy levels, stress levels, and mood, as well as communication, memory, and your immune system. Copious amounts of coffee and energy drinks consumed throughout the day cannot compensate for a lack of sleep. If your body is telling you that it requires more rest, open your heart and honor that information by giving your body what it needs.

What else does your heart need? What does your body need to function optimally? Put your hand over your heart and ask it. Clarissa Pinkola Estes, author of *Women Who Run with the Wolves*, calls the body "the consort": the loyal, sacred part of us that was born to contain the soul; it is our constant companion in this lifetime. She told us that the body loves us and deserves our love in return, though in many places on earth and in many traditional religions, the body is not honored for the valiant work it does. Quite the opposite. It is considered acceptable by some to treat the body badly because it is believed to be a completely separate and lower part of us than the spirit. Because the flesh is considered base and temporary it is acceptable to abuse it or deny it the proper fuel it requires to do its job. "It's alright to forget to eat when the companion is hungry or to stuff the companion with food when the companion is not hungry," Estes explained. She asked us to think of someone we love dearly: ask ourselves what would happen if that person told us that they were hungry or thirsty? Would we ignore that person or dismiss him or her with a gruff, "Yeah, yeah, when I get around to it"? It would be unthinkable.[10]

So what does your body need? More water? More vegetables? Exercise? A warm bath? Time to meditate? Where are you not giving love to yourself? We need to be strong and healthy inside and out to do the work we are being called to do in these times.

How are your relationships? The biggest gift we can give to others is the gift of our focused presence—truly seeing, truly listening to the one before you. When communicating with others, do you speak authentically from your heart? Do you hold on to resentments or release them?

Margaret Mead, the well-known cultural anthropologist, author, and teacher (and my personal mentor), used to practice what she called "freedom of load," where she would consciously release all of the things that were "weighing her down" every evening. This release allowed her to begin the next day full of energy with a fresh, clean outlook, so she could do her work helping people in the world. What is holding you back? Are there people you have not forgiven? Try this forgiveness exercise to free your heart and mind from load.

Process: Forgiveness and Heart Expansion

Sit comfortably in a chair and close your eyes. Breathe deeply in through your nose and out through your mouth several times, relaxing your body more with every breath.

Imagine that you are traveling along a sunlit path through a beautiful forest. Use all of your senses. See the light streaming through the trees. Hear the sound your feet make as they step on the earth; hear the birds overhead. There might be a river nearby. Hear the sound of the water burbling over stones as it rushes along.

The path gently begins to slope downward, and you enter a sunlit clearing. You come to a secret cabin in the woods that is yours alone. You open the door. Everything is in its place. It is simple, but filled with your favorite colors, favorite art pieces, and objects from nature.

There are three chairs facing each other in the center of this pleasant room. Before you sit down, you invite your favorite helpful being from the other side of the veil to join you. This might be Jesus or Mary Magdalene, Kwan Yin or St. Francis, Krishna or the Buddha; whomever you feel will provide the most personal support for you.

This being arrives at the cabin door where you greet him or her warmly and offer a place to sit in one of the three chairs.

Next you invite in the person you are having difficulty forgiving. You greet him or her and offer a place to sit. You then seat yourself in the remaining chair.

With your spiritual partner serving as a silent witness, you ask that all parties communicate from their highest selves and that all that occurs in this space be for the highest good of all.

Turn and share with the person who has offended you all of the feelings that you have about the situation. Don't leave anything out. If you feel like ranting, rant. No need to be polite; pour everything out. Take as much time as you need to do this.

When you have finished and you feel that your side has been completely heard, allow time and space for the other person to express his or her views on same situation. Hear this information with an open heart and from the highest perspective you can. Can you see any way in which this challenging situation might have served your growth or caused you to shift? Offered you an opportunity to become more compassionate? Set stronger boundaries for yourself? Offered you opportunities to look at your self-worth? Could this person sitting across from you have played a part in this challenging scenario as a gift to you in this lifetime?

Continue to dialogue back and forth with the person until you feel some peace about what happened. If you feel the need, you could ask your witness to offer some perspective on the situation as well. When you have finished, thank the person and your witness for coming to help you in this way. Watch them go.

Turn toward the cabin interior and with your hands pour cleansing light energy over the entire space. Exit your cabin and thank it for being available to you whenever you need it.

Move up the gentle slope and along the forest path feeling refreshed. Hear the water in the stream burbling over the stones as it flows along. See the flowers and the patterns the sunlight makes as it filters through the trees and onto the path. Notice how much lighter your heart feels.

Return to the room. When you are ready, open your eyes. You may wish to stretch your body a little bit.

Feeling good, with a balanced heart and mind, you may feel inspired to move your energy out into the world to help others. What these times call for are motivated, intrepid men and women willing to step up and do their part to facilitate this great, positive shift required by this critical time on Earth. You may feel called to become a Social Artist.

So, what is a Social Artist?* Social Artistry is the art of enhancing human capacities in the light of social complexity. It seeks to bring new ways of thinking, being, and doing to social challenges in the world. Social Artistry brings state-of-the-art discoveries in human capacity building to social transformation. The goal of the Social Artist is to build a planetary society based on the principles of democracy, sustainable development, human-based needs and values, universal human rights, environmental protection, social justice, equality, and the sovereignty and dignity of all peoples worldwide.

Social Artists are leaders in many fields who bring to the canvas of our social reality the same order of passion and skill that an artist brings to her art form. It is within the depth work of Social Artistry that we can access the inner capacities to align ourselves with the earth's higher purpose. Ultimately, it is about all of us together cocreating the human and social changes needed to make a better world.

---

* Visit jeanhoustonfoundation.org to learn more.

An organization that is doing just that is the nonprofit Pachamama Alliance, out of San Francisco, dedicated to supporting indigenous people of the rainforest and their natural environment. The Alliance also strives to create a more sustainable, just, and spiritually fulfilling world through education. Lynne Twist, her husband, Bill Twist, and their team have cocreated a powerful symposium called The Awakening the Dreamer Symposium as a way to achieve their objective. In the symposium volunteer presenters explain that we are living in a time of great shift that was predicted long ago in which the people of the Eagle (those who live in the North) come to live in harmony with the people of the Condor (those who live in the South). The people of the Eagle have dominated for five hundred years. Their cultures are more human-centered and intellectual, more technology based and scientific. They *think* things. The cultures of the Condor are more intuitive and heart centered, more in tune with spiritual things. They live close to the Earth in harmony with the environment. It is believed that neither side is superior to the other; both have their value and they have lived separately for too long.[11]

The Achaur tribe in the Ecuadorian Rainforest realized that their world was changing due to encroaching influences from the outside and that they had better make contact with cultures outside of their own if they were going to survive. Contacting Lynne and Bill Twist, they voiced their desire to shift the imbalances they perceived occurring all around them to balances. When the Twists asked the tribe members how they could help, they were told, "If you really want to help us, go back home and change the dream of the North." What this meant in a nutshell was getting Americans and those in other Western cultures to become less materialistic, less competitive, and less domineering over the natural environment. The Twists were up to the task, and the Pachamama Alliance was born.

According to their research, one billion people in this world are living on less than one dollar per day. Two billion people are living on less than two dollars a day, while the three wealthiest people on the planet have more resources than forty-eight nations. The gap between rich and poor has been widening since the 1960s.

At the same time, a global spike in population has occurred. Before 1800, the world's population had remained stable except for a few dips when a plague wiped out great numbers of people in certain areas. In 1800, the population reached one billion. After 1800, with the ability to extract fossil fuels from the earth, there was a tremendous jump in science and industry.[12] Our current world population is well over seven billion.[13] Nearly every natural habitat on the planet is being degraded due to deforestation, pollution, and mass extinction. Every day an average of nineteen species disappears forever.[14] The last time there was a level of extinction this dramatic was in the age of dinosaurs.[15] Species we have taken for granted, such as lions, pandas, polar bears, tigers, and elephants, are teetering on the brink of annihilation forever. Ninety percent of the larger fish that humans eat are already gone.[16] Nearly every person in the scientific community now agrees that we are facing a life-and-death situation—(most professional biologists agree with this, according to a poll taken by the American Museum of Natural History).[17] After reviewing the results of an international study of natural environments that was sponsored by the United Nations, scientists issued a dire warning: *The Earth's ability to sustain life can no longer be taken for granted.*[18] Everything we care about is at stake.

We are currently using more resources than the earth is capable of producing. The people in North America and Western Europe, with our high standard of living, are using the greatest number of resources by far: five Earth's worth of resources per person.

So, what can we do? We created this situation—it is not something being done to us by outside forces—and we can choose something else.

We must examine our previously unexamined assumptions about life. Here are some examples of assumptions held in Western culture:

1. "The earth is a resource here to satisfy my desires for material goods."
2. "This is just a natural cycle we're going through."
3. "Technology will save us."
4. "More is better."
5. "We must continue to expand to make a profit. Progress can only be made through a growing economy."
6. "It's too late to make a change."
7. "I'm only one person. What can I do?"
8. "Everything is renewable."
9. "Everything should evolve around human needs."
10. "We are not connected. Everything is separate."
11. "Other people are the problem, not me."
12. "The planet can always recover."

The people of the Awakening the Dreamer Symposium point out that human beings are not flawed—just mistaken in our thinking. We are not mere consumers; we are so much more than the media and advertisers might have us believe. We are powerful creators living in mythic times, capable of doing anything we set our hearts and minds and courage to. This is not a time to be discouraged. This is not a time to play small.

Consider transformations we once thought would be impossible: the collapse of the Soviet Union; humans landing on the moon; the Arab Spring; the melting of the polar ice caps; the ability to regenerate organs. Who would have thought those things could happen?

The right for women to vote; Gandhi and the power of nonviolent resistance to oust the British Empire from India; Nelson Mandela becoming the president of South Africa after spending twenty-seven years in prison; millions of human beings all over the world connected through handheld cell phones; even the internet and personal, home computers. The fantastic dreams of the past have become the norm. Look around you and notice the ways in which your own community may be shifting. I know that in my own town there is a greater push to consume goods produced locally. We have a farmers' market filled with organic produce and products of humanely raised animals. There is an active recycling movement. A program has been set up wherein bags of groceries may be set up outside one's home and picked up by volunteers for the local food bank.

Around the world car companies aer producing more hybrid cars than ever before. Interfaith movements are springing up; there is a rise in holistic healthcare and the use of alternative forms of energy. Many countries have put restrictions on smoking tobacco products in public places. Most shifts are being made under the radar of the media.

Here is a short excerpt from a poem entitled "Hieroglyphic Stairway" by poet, teacher, activist, and filmmaker Drew Dellinger:

> *It is 3:23 in the morning*
> *And I'm awake*
> *Because my grandchildren*
> *Won't let me sleep.*
> *My great, great grandchildren*
> *Are asking me in the dream*
>
> *What did you do while the planet was plundered?*
> *What did you do while the earth was unraveling?*
> *. . . what did you do*
> *Once you knew?*[19]

E. F. Schumacher said:

Can we rely on it that a "turning around" will be accomplished by enough people quickly enough to save the modern world? This is often asked, but whatever answer is given to it will mislead. The answer "yes" leads to complacency, the answer "no" leads to despair. It is desirable to leave these perplexities behind us and get to work.[20]

The heart of the world is calling for you with your special gifts and unique perspectives. What can you do? What will you do? If each person does something, the whole planet will shift. Sit quietly with your authentic heart and ask the question. It is no accident that you are here at this time. What draws you?

• • • •

Trevelen Rabanal, from East Los Angeles, builds custom motorcycles, hot rods, and low-rider cars. He is best known for his minimalist chopper motorcycles that have won best-of-show awards all over the country, as well as for his appearances on a television series revolving around "custom kulture" and the biker lifestyle. Growing up on the rough streets of East L.A., Trevelen got involved with gangs, drugs, and alcohol at an early age and ended up serving time in the state penitentiary. He explained in a personal interview:

When I was younger I was into wilder things in life and was a real character. Society had no tolerance for my behavior, and I ended up in a correctional facility. I hit bottom and was at the end of my road. I was in twenty-four-hour-a-day lockdown, was a very angry person, and had no reason to be happy.

Then I was given a book of Zen poetry, and I got into Buddhism. Through reading and study, I learned that many people in the world were worse off than I was. I realized that we are all-one-humanity as a whole, but we choose to separate ourselves. I believe that the tools exist to change your life, but it is up to you to acquire them. I realized that I had to fix myself. Upon my release, I didn't want to be involved in anything negative. I believe that all we ever have is the present moment, and I decided to start living in the now and doing something to make a positive difference.

He also adopted the philosophy of his role model His Holiness the Dalai Lama, making Trevelen's religion one of kindness.

Trevelen began studying jujitsu with his other role model, Henry Akins, and also got involved with boxing, yoga, and meditation. This led to the idea of getting kids in gang-torn neighborhoods off the streets and giving them an opportunity to turn their lives around.

He saw teens from broken homes and in heartbreaking situations. He knew that if he could give them an outlet for their aggression, he might be able to help them make a positive change in their lives. Focusing on his desire to help these kids (since he felt they were easier to reach and turn around than adults), he opened the L.A. Boxing Academy with a couple of partners in downtown Los Angeles in 2000. One day, after a thirteen-year-old boy had had a very positive day of training, Trevelen gave him a hug. With tear-filled eyes, the boy admitted that his father had never done that. "I figured that if I could change one kid, I could make a difference," Trevelen confided. "Kids never forget."

The gym attracted kids in East L.A. from rival gangs and neighborhoods. "I knew that if they could get along and train together, work out with each other and coexist in a 3,000 square foot facility, they could learn to stop fighting on the streets."

But opening the gym and keeping it open was no easy task since the city council members didn't want the gym or the kids in their part of the city. "The city council wanted the 'riff-raff' on the other side of the L.A. River," Trevelen remembered. "We were on the wrong side by a few blocks, and the city made it hard for us." He found his battle with the city to be a very culturally biased experience.

"Look, I'm not trying to cure anybody," Trevelen stated, "but a little adjustment on a daily basis can make a difference." So he also started a program at his custom car and motorcycle shop, SuperCo.

We have an open-door policy at SuperCo. I would tell kids to come and see me for thirty days. I would teach them how to work on bikes and cars and listen to them, give them respect. Sometimes that's all it takes.

There was this one kid who came from a really bad neighborhood in Royal Heights. It was a war zone. I taught him how to weld and how to put a motor together. I taught him to ride a motorcycle and how to drive a car. He is a true success story. Today he is a union foreman in the Ironworkers Union. One day we were in the shop and a high-speed chase was on television, which is pretty much a daily occurrence in Los Angeles. We're watching this chase and the kid realized that the bank robbers being chased were his home boys and he tells me, "I'd be in that car right now if it weren't for you."

Trevelen said that the great thing about being recognized as a custom motorcycle builder is that fame opened the door for him to help others. He currently goes into schools and recovery centers to help teens in need and to Alcoholics Anonymous meetings to help kids in recovery. Over the past four years, he let his hair grow long and just recently cut it all off to donate to Locks of Love so they could make a wig for a cancer patient.

Trevelen commented, "Everyone everywhere suffers from something. If I can help, I will. We all have to live here."[21]

• • • •

Ariane Kirtley considers herself to be one ordinary person who felt compelled to do something extraordinary for the people in the Azawak region of Niger. As the daughter of *National Geographic* photographers, Ariane grew up in West Africa, France, and the United States. She attended a Montessori school in Kentucky and an International Baccalaureate high school program in Paris before moving on to Yale, where she studied medical anthropology. She went on to obtain an MA in public health and received a Fulbright scholarship, whereupon she decided to conduct a study in women's health in Niger.

The Azawak region she selected for her study is remote. There are no roads and the nearest health center was a two-day donkey ride away. Ariane had seen poverty before, but she was unprepared for the extreme level of poverty endured by the people of this area. Changing weather conditions had reduced the amount of rainfall they received from five months out of the year to between one and three months—with disastrous results. Pasturelands had dried up, and the formerly nomadic people had become sedentary. People and animals were dying of thirst. Half of all babies born there died of dehydration.

In spite of their desperate circumstances, Ariane found the people were genuinely kind and generous with what little they had, including their last small cup of milk or dirty water, and she bonded with them instantly. Ariane tells the story of her first few hours there. She set up her tent and went to bed; she found the next morning that a goat had been killed to provide her with fresh meat for her breakfast. One of the men in the village had traveled twenty miles by moonlight to obtain the goat so she could eat.

After the rain, it was common practice for the young girls of the village to travel with their donkeys to watering holes up to thirty miles away in order to fill their jugs and bowls with muddy water shared by the animals. In temperatures of 120 degrees Fahrenheit, the open marshes were crowded and the water disappeared quickly, so they dug deeper holes in the contaminated mud to try to tap into water there. It was a dangerous situation. The people of the Azawak could not wash themselves for nine months out of the year. This meant that small injuries or even minor facial blemishes could not be cleaned and therefore became horribly infected.

Determined to help these people, Ariane went to a large international organization dedicated to serving those in need but found no assistance due to the fact that the nomadic people were an ethnic minority the organization did not wish to serve. Even though a good deal of water was discovered beneath the ground (six hundred feet down), the organization believed it would be too difficult and too expensive to reach it. A second international organization gave her the same answer.

With a heavy heart and feeling utterly helpless, Ariane returned home to France and explained the frustrating situation to her husband. No one would help! "Why don't you just do it yourself?" he asked. She was not sure what she could do as one person with no resources, but she called her father in the United States, pouring the story out, crying when she related the number of deaths that were occurring. Her father happened to be sitting in the car beside a woman named Janet Cornelius, a reverend with a huge heart, who immediately wrote a check for $20,000, followed shortly afterward by another check for $100,000 so the first borehole could be made in a place called Tungawashen.

Ariane may have inherited some of her compassion from her father, Michael Kirtley, who started a nonprofit organization named Friendship Caravan dedicated to cultivating closer relationships between Muslims and Americans after the 9/11 terrorist attacks on the twin towers of the World Trade Center in 2001. Michael introduced his daughter to a humanitarian friend of his, Andrew Kutt, the peace-loving head of the Oneness-Family School (based in the Montessori philosophy) in Chevy Chase, Maryland. Ariane was invited to share photos and her story at the school where she met Debbie Kahn, a school administrator. Debbie confided to me in a personal interview that she had had no idea she would become a humanitarian, but Ariane's passion and dedication to the people dying of thirst in Niger stirred her heart so much that she ended up quitting her position at the school and devoting herself to this new cause—Amman Imman (Water Is Life)—full time.

Andrew Kutt and Debbie Kahn invited Ariane to speak at an international Montessori conference in Florida, and she poured out her story to the teachers there. There was not a dry eye in the room after the presentation, and the inspired teachers brainstormed ways they could get their individual schools to help bring water to the Azawak. Debbie started a blog to keep interested parties apprised of the progress of over sixty Montessori schools from around the world who were raising money to create Wells of Love through Amman Imman. A borehole was drilled in the village of Kijigari and officially dubbed Montessori Well of Love because the donations were collected by the children themselves after coming up with ingenious fund-raising ideas. They put on plays, held neighborhood carnivals, set up lemonade stands, sold their toys in garage sales, and held walkathons. Montessori preschool children as young as three years old made bookmarks and sold them. One Girl Scout troop placed images of the people of Niger on baby-food jars that they then placed beside every water source in their houses. When a dish was washed or a toilet flushed or teeth brushed, the person using the water dropped pennies, dimes, and nickels into the jars and the families were reminded of how easy it was for them to turn on a tap to get all the water they needed while their brothers and sisters across the world did not have that luxury. Debbie created kid-friendly presentations that students could download from the internet by themselves, and children as young as second grade made moving presentations to their classmates.

When Ariane returned to the people of the Azawak region with letters and handmade cards drawn by the Montessori children, even the men of the village were so touched and filled with gratitude that they cried to think that youngsters on the other side of the planet cared so much about them. It took tremendous heart and courage to build boreholes for these people. Ariane's husband traveled to Niger to supervise the construction of one of the wells, and armed guards were required at some points due to political unrest.

At the time of this writing, Ariane is the mother of a four-year-old and has a baby on the way. Both Ariane and Debbie are quick to mention that neither of them knows anything about business. Everything they do for Amman Imman is on a volunteer basis; their nonprofit work is run out of Debbie's home. They are not independently wealthy, nor are they in prestigious political positions of power. They saw a problem and knew they had to do something tangible to help. Debbie says that she feels much more grounded and connected to the earth since starting this project. She says the sense of need has given her an opportunity to be generous and compassionate; she feels much more like a whole person now.

As they moved forward, doors opened and connections were made. Enough money was raised to drill another borehole in the village of Ebagueye in February 2012. The boreholes have provided piping and separate running water faucets for the humans and the animals of these places. The flow of water means that village women and children could plant gardens, and a school was built. Lives were completely transformed by the compassionate hearts and hard work of these two women and the many families who wanted to bring hope to a region that had been past hope.[22]

• • • •

Trevelen Rabanal, Ariane Kirtley, and Debbie Kahn are examples of three Social Artists who opened their hearts, saw what needed to be done, and took action to make a difference. On her Hero's Journey to the Emerald City, Dorothy, too, acts with an open heart and does what needs to be done for her companions. Upon meeting the Tin Man and hearing of his troubles, neither the Scarecrow nor Dorothy hesitates a moment in asking him if he would like to join their quest to see the wonderful Wizard of Oz for a brain and a way to return home to Kansas. They explain that perhaps the Wizard would also give the Tin Man the heart he feels he lacks. Delighted, the man of tin links arms with his new friends and with a merry song they head off to new adventures on the winding Yellow Brick Road. Through the trials that follow, as you might imagine, the Tin Man proves to be the most emotionally wise and sympathetic of Dorothy's allies.

6

THE COURAGE TO BE

Imagine that you are in Dorothy's shoes for a moment. Within the first fifteen minutes of your arrival in this mysterious place, you find yourself face-to-face with one of the scariest villains ever seen. This apparently evil witch has appeared in a blaze of sulfur and smoke, and she begins to make trouble. How frightening is this creature? For starters, her skin is green. A very intense shade of green. Unlike the rainbow-colored garb worn by the cheerful Munchkins and the cotton-candy frock of the Good Witch of the North, this furious witch is dressed to impress in flowing, dramatic black. Her laser-sharp focus is zeroed in on your destruction. And obtaining those glittering ruby slippers that are glued to your feet. The witch disappears as quickly as she arrives (and just as dramatically), in a towering column of fire. Heaven only knows when or where the creature may reappear.

Imagine that you have been informed that the only way to escape a horrible fate at the hands of this witch is to travel quite a distance to a mysterious place called The Emerald City to meet with a powerful Wizard who may (but possibly will not) be able to help you find a way back to your own dimension. You are told that you must walk alone along a Yellow Brick Road, without aid or GPS and with no cell phone. And you had better get going before that scary witch returns. Best of luck, kid.

It is very difficult to imagine the kind of intestinal fortitude it would take to stop quivering in those ruby slippers in order to take even the first step along that path of yellow bricks. But plucky little Dorothy from Kansas takes a deep breath, squares her shoulders, and with only a tail-wagging cairn terrier for protection, sets off into an unknown and utterly strange realm of wonders and horrors. Could you do it? Could you skip merrily down that golden path, off the edge of reality, singing with gusto? Or would you run back into your crushed house and lie shivering under what is left of your bed, hoping it will all just go away?

Courage is a major theme of both the book and the movie. Though the focus is primarily on the famous Cowardly Lion and his desire to acquire the elusive attribute, each of the characters on this shared journey displays tremendous courage numerous times, and always in service to others.

Shortly after the freshly oiled Tin Man joins the group, the travelers come to a dark and ominous wood. Their pace slows as they move through this overgrown part of the forest, but they are determined and do not turn back. Dorothy wonders aloud what dangerous animals might lurk in this unwholesome place, and the Tin Man suggests that perhaps the only creatures to fear might be "Lions and tigers and bears! Oh my!" The allies cling to one another even more tightly and press forward.

As often happens in life, that which we resist persists so, naturally, at that very moment the girl from Kansas and her new friends find themselves face-to-face with an aggressive, roaring lion that has lunged forth from behind a rock to attack them. The frightening beast circles and begins to bully the group of travelers with snarls and threats.

The lion chases poor Toto around and around until finally the dog leaps into Dorothy's arms. The exasperated girl is filled with the compassionate courage borne of one who cannot stand seeing someone bigger picking on someone who is not his own size and, without thinking, she slaps the lion on the nose. The lion bursts into tears and all of his bravado immediately disintegrates. He is a cowardly lion indeed, afraid of his own shadow, afraid even of the mice in the forest.

Once the girl stands up to him, the lion admits that what he lacks is courage and, like the Tin Man and the Scarecrow before him, he launches into a song that explains his predicament and what he might achieve if he "only had the nerve."[1]

Feeling sorry for him, Dorothy invites the Cowardly Lion to join the group of travelers. She explains that she and her allies are on a journey to the Emerald City to meet with the wonderful Wizard of Oz to get a brain, a heart, and a way home. She tells him that perhaps the Wizard could help him get some courage as well. The lion accepts this offer and, of course, even though he is afraid, he will eventually leap chasms, battle the dreaded flying monkeys, and proves to be the very model of courage.

What do you think of when you imagine a courageous person? Someone who wades into a dangerous situation selflessly to, say, rescue a child from a burning building? That may be true, but before we go any further, please take a look in the mirror. The most courageous thing you've ever done is agree to be born on this planet. Congratulate yourself that you've made it to this point in your life; you couldn't have done it without courage. In fact, you are courageous every time you get out of bed in the morning, put on your clothes, and head out the door. It is a profound job to be here.

For most of us, such attributes as compassion and courage are revealed in times of great adversity, those times when we are tested to see what we are made of. We find out much about our own moral compass when we are given a situation in which we must stand up for ourselves or for others: standing up to a bully at school, standing up to authority, standing up for those less fortunate, and being a voice of hope where no voice is speaking out.

Julia Butterfly Hill, author of *The Legacy of Luna*, is best known for living in a 180-foot-tall, 1,500-year-old California Redwood for an amazing 738 days in order to prevent loggers of the Pacific Lumber Company from cutting it down. She said, "Real courage is the space when ordinary becomes extraordinary; it exists when any person faces fears and insecurities and chooses to act anyway."[2]

For our friend the Cowardly Lion, facing and overcoming fears and insecurities is proof that you've got "the nerve." Interestingly, the very people you read about in the newspaper or see on the television news or on the internet, the people who stood up for something or dared to save someone when others just stood by, frozen by apathy, are our neighbors, members of our community. And sometimes they are us.

When asked why they ran into that burning building or pulled that child out of a raging river or stood up to brutality in the name of equality, everyday heroes often respond, "I didn't think; I just did what I felt was right."

Stories of courage have the ability to shake things up and inspire us to live in an expanded way. One needn't climb Mount Everest or jump out of a perfectly good airplane in order to test one's mettle. Emotional and mental courage can be every bit as challenging. It can sometimes be as difficult as saying, "I forgive you."

Courage is about stepping into your grander self, your bigger story. What are your fears, and where do you find that you limit yourself? Are you afraid of standing out, of being noticed? Perhaps you are afraid of making the wrong decision. What are the limiting beliefs that keep you from stepping into your bigger, courageous self?

In her excellent book *Those Who Dare: Real People, Real Courage*, author Katherine Martin asked us to consider where we choose to limit ourselves:

One way we keep ourselves small is by thinking we're not good enough. We're not smart enough, not gregarious enough, not witty enough, not savvy enough, not pretty enough, not educated enough, not clever enough, not romantic enough endlessly not enough. When rooted in childhood these feelings of not being enough can come from parents, teachers, authority figures, cliques we never belonged to, kids we wanted to be like, or friends who dumped us. Somewhere inside us are dreams and desires we haven't made good on because that little gnat keeps buzzing around our heads: "You're not smart enough to do that" or "You're not clever enough; are you kidding?" or "You're not experienced enough for that!" What does your gnat have to say? What about you isn't good enough? Who told you that? What does it kept you from doing?[3]

She went on to pose this question: "Imagine what you could do if you knew, without a doubt, that you were enough. What would you do?"[4]

Stephen Diamond offered ways to tap into your inner hero:

Courage is required in almost every basic human activity or endeavor. For instance, to allow oneself to love and commit to another person takes immense courage. Separating from our parents and forging an independent life for ourselves is a courageous act. To survive an abusive, traumatic or neglected childhood with some sense of dignity and integrity intact demonstrates tremendous courage and resilience.[5]

Diamond also reminded us that it takes courage to be authentically oneself in the world, to be truly creative and artistically express one's innermost self. Career and relationship changes require great courage, as does following a dream.

One of the things that the Cowardly Lion teaches us in *The Wizard of Oz* is that courage is not synonymous with being fearless. The Lion is scared nearly out of his skin by his environment and all of those living things in it. In order to present himself to Dorothy and her allies, he chooses to puff himself up in a show of great bravado to mask his insecurity and downright fear of any newcomer that happens by his little piece of the woods.

Here we all learn that the Lion's blowhard bravado is merely an act to hide his insecurity and fear. Later, he must rise above his fears in order to stand before the great Wizard, though his knees are shaking terribly. He must persevere in the quest to find the Wicked Witch of the West when he and his comrades traverse a haunted forest filled with all sorts of scary things, including invisible ghosts with the power to lift the Tin Man off his feet.

If all this were not enough, the Lion must then steel his resolve to climb an impossible mountain, overcome his fears, trick the Witch's armed guards, don a disguise that doesn't quite cover him, enter into the very heart of the witch's castle of darkness to rescue Dorothy, and defeat the powerful magic of the evil creature who lives there.

Having succeeded in the impossible task of bringing the broomstick of the Wicked Witch back to the Emerald City, the Lion must then hold his own before the billowing smoke, fire, and bellowing of the Wizard once again. He must courageously speak up for Dorothy and his friends when it looks like the Wizard is going to renege on his offer to help them.

Through all of this, the Cowardly Lion is afraid for his life and literally shaking in his fur, but he goes on. He goes on when there is little hope of success and when doom seems imminent at every turn. It is this going forth against all odds that is the heart of courage. (The word *courage* derives from the Latin *cor* or the French *coeur*, meaning "heart," so one could say that courage is a matter of heart.)

You may currently be faced with a challenging situation where you must become as brave as the Cowardly Lion or the other characters of our story. It could be a matter of changing something in your life that is no longer working, confronting someone, or stepping forward to achieve a dream or goal against odds that seem insurmountable. Here is a process to help you move through the fear and into the part of yourself that knows what to do. This can be used for personal issues or to move forward into daunting big projects you wish to accomplish.

Process: Gathering Courage

You need drawing materials of your choice, a large piece of blank paper, and a smaller piece of blank paper.

When you wish to feel courageous, good posture helps. During this exercise (and in any situation where courage may be required), keep your spine straight and at the same time keep the body relaxed and receptive.

Sit at a table with your feet firmly placed on the ground. Relax your muscles with intention and breathe deeply into your belly. Inhale through your nose and exhale through your mouth. Do this several times.

Honor that part of your magnificent brain that has always worked to keep you safe. It has done its job well.

Take a moment to thank your ancestors for getting you here. None of them were careless people, or you wouldn't exist. You come from a long line of courageous people! Acknowledge that.

When you are ready, draw a picture of yourself in the center of the larger piece of paper. Make yourself colorful and BIG—not small. Leave room to write between your image and the margins of the paper. You might be wearing armor or radiating light— whatever image serves you and portrays your inner strength and courage.

Close to the body you have drawn, surround yourself with colorful words or pictures that describe all the positive inner qualities you like best about yourself. For example, you might write, "I am a loving person" or "I get good ideas" or "I finish what I begin." When you write something down or create an image of it, that thing becomes real to the mind and body. You are giving it power and attention.

Next, create a layer of words or images illustrating all of your allies, seen and unseen. (Yes, your dog or cat counts.)

Outside of these layers, list or illustrate some of the large and small challenges you have had in the past that you have overcome. How did you show courage? Remember the strength and power you felt in those times. This reminds your mind and body that you have been previously successful in your endeavors. Bring the feelings that you had once the situation was resolved back into your consciousness as well. Let them flood your blood and bones.

On the smaller piece of paper, draw an image of the person or situation that is currently challenging you.

Around this image write down or draw all of the ways in which you feel blocked by this person or thing. With your mighty brain, heart, and courage, take each of the items you have drawn or written one by one and come up with a possible solution. Have a ready rebuttal for each negative aspect of the problem. Bring in your love and compassion. Ask yourself some key questions. Do you need more allies to help you? Who are they? Contact them. Are there skills you could hone or acquire that might assist you in overcoming this challenge? Write these things down, too.

Think of someone whose courage you greatly admire. It might be Mahatma Gandhi or Mother Teresa, Hillary Clinton, Koichi Nakagawa, Rosa Parks, Caesar Chavez, or Nelson Mandela. It could be Dr. Haing S. Ngor, Crazy Horse, or even someone from your own family or a personal friend. Imagine that person standing in front of you now. Present your problem to this person and ask how he or she would handle it. Write down the answers.

This is a step-by-step process. Breaking the information down into bite-size chunks makes it easier to accomplish. What can you do to move forward in this moment? Trust yourself to respond appropriately. Courage grows through acts of courage. Celebrate each positive step you take.

Before you finish this exercise, write on the top of the page that holds your shining, colorful image, "Yes! Of course I can do it!" And believe it, because, of course, you can.

Any time that you need to call up your courage, remember to ground yourself physically by planting both feet on the ground while keeping the body straight and strong but also soft and receptive. Widen and sharpen your sense of awareness. Expand your energy field—not in aggression, for that only escalates aggression toward you, but in strength—while decreasing your fear. Breathe deeply from your belly. Listen to your heart. Be authentic and calm in your actions and reactions. Call upon your invisible allies to help you. Trust yourself and the Universe. Ask yourself, "Can I safely stand up to this person (or whatever is challenging you)?" Gently push the boundaries of your bravery out. Incremental advancement is wonderful—no need to shake the earth overnight, but I would urge you to think big, not small. Be bold.

The part of our brains that protected us in ancient times from snakes and the dark and other dangers is still in operation, yet we have different kinds of everyday challenges today. We need to assure those places in our brains that we are safe when confronted with the realities of our modern times that are not life threatening.

Courage is being called forth in us now more than ever. We must do what we can do in each moment. We need to muster our strength and pull together our physical, mental, emotional, and spiritual resources. We must be creative and resourceful, and we must have endurance. This is the time for our voices to be heard. Do you strongly believe in something? Can you stand up for it? Speak up? Write about it? Is there some positive action you can take right now?

Throughout every step of Dorothy's journey in the magical Land of Oz, she is given choices. Should she continue along the Yellow Brick Road when situations get tough? When she is tired or hungry? Should she run away? Defend Toto? Let Toto fend for himself? Fight the witch? Give up? Speak up to the Wizard? Be silent? We are blessed as human beings to have the power of choice. We choose how we use our energy and the hours of each day. Every choice you make has an effect on something else; we are all connected. What do you choose?

Chris Fontana is the executive director of Global Visionaries in Seattle, Washington, an organization dedicated to creating true global citizens through leadership training and work with high school students of different ethnic and economic backgrounds. Diverse groups of students selected to participate in the program study Spanish and Guatemalan culture for many months before taking a two-week trip to Guatemala, where they live with a local family and work on a specific project they have chosen. That work might include planting trees in an area that has been deforested or helping to build a new school alongside local residents. It might include spending time in a hospital with the elderly or disabled patients who live there full-time, holding their hands and sharing stories. Sometimes it involves working with Guatemalan families who make their living growing and selling coffee.

With free-trade and even fair-trade practices, the farmers receive only a shockingly small percentage of the total cost of the coffee when it is sold in stores. In fact, it is such a small amount that they can never really get ahead financially. Some Global Visionary students participate in a direct-trade program where they transport, roast, package, and sell the coffee themselves. This results in a far greater percentage of the profits going to the farmers. The students benefit as well, for they are able to use their share of the profits to fund their trip to Guatemala.

The students claim that seeing the way people of other cultures live in the world helps to give them an expanded perspective. They often return to the United States feeling less of a need to accumulate material possessions and more of a desire to help others and the environment. Some students have difficulty fitting back in with friends stateside who have not made the journey.

• • • •

Chris Fontana started college with a desire to teach Spanish to high school students in his hometown of Chicago. In his junior year, he studied in Spain, which changed his idea of who he was and how he lived as an American. He started teaching in the public schools and found himself one day after Thanksgiving with no lesson plan. The bell rang, signaling the start of class, and Chris decided on the spot to talk about current events in South America. In that class the high school freshmen became outraged after learning that industrialized countries were cutting down the Amazon rainforest at a rate of one and a half acres per second, and they decided to take immediate action. They started an ecology club and wanted their school to begin recycling, but the administrators responded by informing the students that such a program was not necessary. The teachers and custodians took the students' side, and for two weeks they all secretly saved and storing in cupboards the used paper that accumulated in the class-rooms. At the end of two weeks, the students placed the mountain of paper in the middle of the cafeteria and called the newspapers to cover the event. A brand-new recycling program was implemented in the school immediately afterward.

Chris comes from a family of teachers, and in 1992 he and his brother Joe Fontana, along with Jason Foster, one of Joe's highly moti-vated students, decided to create a Youth Environmental Summit similar to the international Earth Summit that had been held for adults in Rio de Janeiro that same year. Jason helped to organize the summit along with other high school students, which included raising money and signing up speakers. In the years that followed, they held two suc-cessful youth summits that were well attended by young people from forty states and thirty-two countries. The summits gave participants and organizers a feeling of deep connection with the world and also a feeling that they could do anything. Following that experience, Jason

Foster backpacked around the world for a year, returning with the idea of creating Global Visionaries. Chris and Joe thought it was a fabulous idea and hopped on board. (Jason went on to become an attorney and currently works for the United Nations.)

Global Visionaries is run in a democratic fashion that empowers students. The teens who return from Guatemala have the option of returning the following year to mentor newcomers. Students engage in fund-raising projects throughout the year in order to pay for their own trip expenses and to make a donation to the Guatemalan people they want to help. Throughout their training period, students in Seattle make friends with other teens from areas outside their own neighborhoods and ethnic backgrounds, thus expanding their understanding and cooperation skills.

Chris learned the power of people working together toward a common goal when he was a child. His mother raised her energetic family of eight in a unique way when she decided to bring democracy to the household. They held meetings regularly, and the children's voices were heard and honored. All jobs were distributed evenly and no one could go out and play until the work was done. Chris laughs when he mentions that he was cooking family dinners for eight people by the time he was in second grade. If friends came over, they were also given chores to do. Some of them had never operated a vacuum before! There was a strong sense of unity in this family because of these practices. Chris wanted to bring this philosophy and feeling of shared accomplishment to his students in the Global Visionaries program.

Chris admits that when he began the organization he had no business skills, little money, and few contacts. His only support came from friends, family, and the parents of some of his students, but that did not hinder him. "No one is ever ready until they start," he says. "Life begins at the edge of your comfort zone." He suggests that the best way to avoid getting overwhelmed or depressed about the state of the world is to take action:

> Keep alive the possibility that you could actually achieve your dream. Action keeps me optimistic and that affects the outcome. Even when mistakes are made along the way, I keep saying "It's going to work out! It's going to work out!" And somehow it does. When I began this work I tended to think I had to do it all, but I found out that that attitude can quickly lead to burnout. Let other people contribute. Let them do what they're good at and enjoy doing.

If he does feel burned out or lost occasionally, Chris taps into mentors in the community and asks for their support. He used to think that lack of money was the biggest obstacle to achieving his goals for the organization, but he now feels that problems can be solved by staying connected to the community, to people and creative resources. "It's people who make the difference. For a number of years we did a bunch of work with no money," he says. This service-oriented group is creating peace on earth, social justice through education, and hands-on experience because a few dedicated people with a life-altering vision had the heart and courage to put their dreams for a better world into action.[6]

• • • •

Worldwide, societies are crying for assistance in the transformation of their citizens, organizations, and institutions. New ways of looking at leadership are required, as well as new methods of developing coura-geous human beings eager to serve humanity. Leaders in this new world are now required to work cocreatively *with* their constituents, thus discontinuing models of dependency and social apathy.

Thirty years of work throughout the world with leaders in the fields of industry and government, education and health has convinced me that too many of the problems in societies today stem from leadership that is ill prepared to deal with present complexity. This is not just a matter of inadequate training in the realities of global change but, even more tragically, a lack of human resourcefulness, leaders living out of a field of awareness that limits their abilities to deal with their world. Too many leaders have been educated for a different time, a different world. Few are prepared for the task of dealing with the complexity and chaos of today when the usual formulas and stopgap solutions of an earlier era will not help. We must begin to help people, citizens and leaders alike, to bring new mind to bear upon social change. In this way it is hoped that we can rise to the challenge of our times and ferry ourselves across the dangerous abyss that separates a dying era from a new Renaissance.

The work of Social Artistry is evolving and open-ended, striving to provide a dynamic balance between inner understanding and outward expression. The Social Artist is one who brings the focus, perspective, skill training, tireless dedication, and fresh vision of the artist to the social arena. Thus the Social Artist medium is the human community. They seek innovative solutions to troubling conditions and are lifelong learners ever-hungry for insights, skills, imaginative ideas, and deeper understanding of present-day issues. Social Artists are intimately familiar with the cultures of the places where they choose to work. They take the time to learn the stories, customs, and at least some of the language with an enthusiastic, positive attitude.

People who agree to this challenge have the maturity, initiative, and vision as well as the passion for making a difference in the whole domain of human affairs. They have done their inner homework. It requires considerable mind, heart, and courage to take up this work, for what is being formed is possibly a movement as profound as it is out-reaching in its implications for proactive social evolution.

Oftentimes the work of Social Artists around the world requires a great deal of fearlessness and fortitude since working in newly emerging countries and areas of civil unrest and severe poverty can be an extremely dangerous experience. This was certainly the case in 2002 when Monica Sharma, director of Leadership and Capacity Development for the United Nations; Jan Sanders, an American Social Artist; and Tatwa Timsina, head of the Institute of Cultural Affairs in Nepal (ICA Nepal) decided to create HIV/AIDS workshops during a time of great civil unrest in a war-torn region where over fourteen thousand people had been killed. Though they had been told that the area was too unstable and dangerous to enter, the three Social Artists were determined about their mission. In 2004, Tatwa participated in the Social Artistry Institute's Training Program, and in 2008 he set out to create a training session in Nepal in which one hundred people came together in the eastern part of Nepal to stem the tide of an AIDS epidemic. Many participants came through checkpoints and were beaten up on the way to the meeting, but they continued on. Despite the challenges, twenty facilitators were specifically trained in Social Artistry leadership techniques at that meeting. They took the teachings they learned back to their communities, and the program became a model for other AIDS programs. It was an example of true leadership in action at a time when many people had given up all hope of helping the region.

• • • •

Durga was one of the twenty Social Artist facilitators who came out of this training. He saw a special way to help the people of Nepal. In this incredibly impoverished land, most of the men must leave home to find work in other regions in order to make money for their families and villages. Durga had no budget but decided to teach the people of one village to grow organic food. He got a small grant for a two-year plan, rolled up his sleeves, and started planting.

Soon, people of the area were raising organic vegetables, and Durga created a farmers' market in a town some fifty miles away. The fresh produce was trucked to the market and, soon profits from this farming project changed the lives of the entire village. For the first time ever, men could return to live and work the land of their own village with their families. Durga's plan was extended, and for over five years, he has been working to change the face of poverty and famine. He has offered pride and hope to a forgotten people. Durga's work has become a model for organic farming in Nepal, and his plan has been success-fully replicated in many other areas of that country.[7]

• • • •

Tales of transformation and courage by everyday people like this often inspire courage in our own lives. Katherine Martin, author of *Those Who Dare: Real People, Real Courage*, shared many inspiring stories of people from all walks of life who have dared to do things that have changed their own lives, the lives of those in their immediate families, their communities and, in some cases, the world. Sometimes these are stories in which the men or women involved don't even realize that they are acting with courage.

Martin related the story of Mark Nyberg, a missionary from Oregon who literally put his life on the line to save the children of an orphanage during the collapse of Albania in 1997. While most Americans in the area of Vlora evacuated due to the extreme levels of violence, Mark stayed on to save the kids he loved from looters, the local mafia, and the child slavery market.

After seven months of chaos, Albania was able to restore a kind of peace. However, during those seven months, every institution in the city had been attacked and ransacked: the hospitals, the children's clinics, everything except the orphanage Mark had guarded with his life and one other orphanage that had been guarded by brave men Mark had sent over to do the job. He said, "My staying in Albania wasn't so much an act of courage as an act of love. During the uprising, I kept thinking, if this were different, if it were my own children in my own home, I'd do the same thing. That's the power of love."[8]

Millions of people right now are experiencing a yearning and a desire to awaken to their unique gifts and offer them in service to the world while at the same time living a life of joy and fulfillment. It's a surging of the human spirit, a virtual global awakening on a scale that no one has seen before. Simply put, people are longing to finally feel fully alive and to step into their unique purpose in life. It takes courage to be who you really are and to do what you came to do!

So, why is living a life of meaning and purpose so difficult? It is because our current social systems have not been set up to prepare us to live a life of true purpose. Today's culture exists not to nurture our highest aspirations, but to ensure our basic survival.

Our educational system is designed to create good workers who will slot into jobs and careers—not to empower fiery, creative people who are forging the path ahead together. Our social contracts exist to perpetuate the status quo—not to encourage our highest potentials to blossom. Is it any wonder why so many people's best attempts to evolve themselves and our culture fall short of the goal? We simply haven't been trained in how to bring the possible future into the present.

We can no longer afford to become overwhelmed by all the changes going on in the world around us. We have outgrown the small story of our lives and the small selves to which so many have confined themselves. It is time to acknowledge that the Universe resides within us. It is time to embrace higher ways of being for a new era. It is time to move through life motivated not by guilt or obligation but by gratitude and an abiding zest for doing the things that are called forth by living out of our higher purpose.

What happens when we do this? As Dorothy tells us as she sings "Over The Rainbow," "the dreams that you dare to dream, really do come true."[9] So it is that we find ourselves with Dorothy on her journey along the Yellow Brick Road with her faithful allies—representations of the mind, heart, courage, and the ever-faithful life force energy in the form of Toto. Together they are ready to step into the next phase of the Hero's Journey.

The friends look across wide-open fields and there it is, rising up before them in the distance: the glittering towers of the Emerald City. With renewed excitement, the friends charge forward, eager to reach their goal and eager to meet the wonderful Wizard of Oz at last.

7

FALLING ASLEEP
IN FIELDS OF POPPIES

From a high tower in her dark stone castle, the Wicked Witch observes the progress of Dorothy and her friends through the magic of her crystal ball. She sees how close they are to reaching their objective and decides to cast a spell over the group so they can never make it. With mortar and pestle and a wave of her bony green hands, she conjures up a nasty potion: "Something with poison in it, but attractive to the eye and soothing to the smell"—lush fields of poppies that stretch out in all directions as far as the eye can see. The beautiful flowers appear directly in front of the travelers and are so thick that they cover the Yellow Brick Road. The witch knows that the poppies will put them to sleep and their journey will end. As the unsuspecting companions race across the field, Dorothy, Toto, and the Cowardly Lion, who are all made of flesh and blood, suddenly become exhausted. They advance more and more slowly until they cannot take a single step more. Overcome, they tumble down amid the flowers to sleep.

This is the danger zone. How many projects have foundered at the threshold of accomplishment because people got lax and lost vigilance? Human beings tend to get sleepy or fall into apathy when they get close to their goals. Why does this happen? What are the things that block us?

It takes a lot of energy to stay on the path, and the diversions of this world are strong. We may feel alone or physically exhausted. It may seem as though we are not making progress fast enough, or we may feel that there's too much to do. When we feel helpless or hopeless, it is so easy to switch on the television and let the flickering screen take us away. We may immerse ourselves in computer games, rush to the mall to buy something we don't need, or turn to food or drugs or alcohol for comfort. We slip into our old ways of being because forward motion simply takes too much effort. Our paths are covered with seductive poppies that seem like quick fixes, but in reality are working to neutralize our senses, numb our creativity, and dull our drive.

Many people have woken up, have heard the call to expand internally, and wish to create positive shifts to help the earth and humanity, but they frequently find resistance from others who want their friend, spouse, or coworker to simply go back to sleep and maintain the status quo. When one person changes, the others in relationship with that person must change also, and that can be a problem. The energized person who has outgrown his or her old life template may find that the struggle with others who are not ready to grow in that way is so challenging that it is simply easier to slide back into old patterns rather than continue on the new path. Is there anyone in your life you feel is holding you back from being who you really are? Transformation requires energy and commitment. It is not always easy. Many people give up and allow the entropy monster to suck the life out of them.

So often in my work with people all over the world I hear, "I'm only one person, Jean. What can I do?" The challenges of this world feel like they are closing in, and we may feel helpless against the deluge of perceived troubles. That's why it is so important to have others who will not fall asleep available to wake you up and keep you on your path.

As we discussed in chapter 4, our brains are actually wired with mirror neurons that respond when we observe others taking an action, as if we were taking the action ourselves. Researchers at the University of Parma in the early 1990s made this exciting discovery while studying the brain function of macaque monkeys. They noticed that when a monkey merely observed a scientist cracking open and eating nuts, a section of her brain fired as if she were engaging in the opening and eating of the nuts herself. When an action was perceived by one monkey, mirror neurons were triggered within the brains of other monkeys, creating a vicarious experience as if all the monkeys had physically taken the action. Further research related to this topic of mirror neurons has revealed that human beings understand others not by thinking but by feeling. We are empathic creatures, connected to others through this marvelous facet of our brains.[1]

By observing vital, activated people around us, we become activated ourselves. If we surround ourselves with those who wish to remain sleeping, chances are good that we will remain sleeping also. Reflect for a moment on who supports you in this lifetime. Do you have a community of beloveds ready and willing to shake you and wake you, should you fall asleep? An ongoing teaching and learning community is essential in doing the work you are called to do. If you do not have a community that serves your needs by energizing and encouraging you, then create one. And if some members of your group fall into apathy or entropy from time to time, you can take your turn and wake them up. The key is to be there for each other as you move toward a common purpose.

When Dorothy, Toto, and the Cowardly Lion slip into slumber so close to their goal, the faithful Scarecrow and Tin Man try to rouse them. Seeing their predicament, Glinda the Good Witch casts a powerful spell of her own to counteract the effects of the Wicked Witch's dark magic. Gently falling snow awakens the sleepers.

Cultivating a daily, ever-deepening relationship with your entelechy also keeps you awake in rough times. Remember that the Great Friend yearns for you as much as you yearn for it. Taking time to cultivate that mutual connection ensures that the wisdom from that Source is always readily available to you. Take time each morning and or evening to quiet your mind and open your heart to this powerful energy within you. Ask questions and write down any answers that come to you. Ask and you shall receive.

There are other issues that slow our progress or keep us stuck. So frequently I hear people mention that the lack of money is what keeps them from taking action in their lives. The issue of money seems to consume the lives of so many people. Let's take a look at that.

Years ago, I read John Kenneth Galbraith's *The Affluent Society* and was struck to the core when he characterized so well the present economic structure in America as based not only on the satisfaction of desire but on the creation of desire. This is virtually unique in the history of the economies of most cultures, and Galbraith concluded that the creation of desire creates the need for more production of goods and services, which generates loss of connection to the true things in life. He went on to say, "Production only fills a void that it has itself created."[2]

I think we all agree that money has become more important than ever. As Galbraith suggested half a century ago, it pervades society in every possible way, and that is true much more now than ever in any other civilization. Everything becomes monetized. There was a time when issues involving personal relationships, doctors and medicine, academic relationships, or artistic life were considered out of the realm of monetary measures. An artist could be appreciated for who he was without being financially successful. A doctor was willing to perform a medical treatment without necessarily being paid right away or even at all, if the patient could not afford to pay. Now, however, if people talk about disease, often the healthcare cost is an important part of the current discussion. For example, the fact that tobacco companies have to pay billions of dollars in damages seems more important than the deaths and diseases caused by tobacco. Everything is being priced nowadays, and this shows how money has entered every corner of our lives. Part of this development has to do with the breakdown of values in our culture. Money has come in to fill this gap.

Instead of killing each other, we sue each other. The power of money is that it has started quantifying life, but it takes away the qualitative aspects of life. That coincides with another development in our culture, that we use our mind more and our heart less when making decisions.

In spite of all the progress and accomplishments we can make that have come with the affluent society, often it appears that our Western culture seems to favor the diminishing of our being. More and more we are less and less consciously present in the present, because we feel instead that we must be available to the things and jobs we are asked to perform. Both the ancient Greeks and the Hebrews regarded the land of Hades and the world of Sheol as the place of shadows, forgetfulness, and the diminishment of being. And Hades at least is the land of Pluto, the place of great wealth. Too many today regard their existence as hellish because they are without presence, without significance, without meaning. That is why it is so important to try to understand the place of money in our lives.

In all the great cultures of the past, there was nothing like the immense global mechanism of finance, whose penetration into every aspect of human life has been the chief feature of our modern culture. Today, money is the goal, which means that the expenditure of human energy, which in the past went to quality of life, now goes to the acquisition of money and the security it represents. And we also have been sold a lie that creates a brain glitch, one that persuades us we cannot have happiness without a ton of money. So we work all the time or fret all the time to have the money to do the things we want, and we end with the sense of insufficiency at every level.

One of the biggest forms of our insufficiency is what we might term *time poverty*. What do I mean by this? I noted that the proliferation of desire has been the basis for our capitalistic economy. It is not the satisfaction of desire but the creation of artificial desire. People do not need 99 percent of the products that are offered in the marketplace. If the so-called normal desires were to be satisfied, the economy would collapse. The economy is based upon delusions and false desires. You recall that then-president George W. Bush declared after the terrorist attacks of 9/11 that the solution to our fears was to go shopping. Shopping! We laughed, but there was a horrible truth to his inane statement. If America is not to collapse after the terrorist attack, we have to return to its core reality, which is, apparently, shopping.

Who needs twenty kinds of orange juice in the supermarket? This is where the time problem comes in. Because of all these desires, we have to work harder and longer hours to afford these desires, and as a result we have too little time to buy the products or services, let alone enjoy them. This, in turn, is a reflection of living in our heads and continuously being busy with our possible future desires. Time seems to pass faster and faster. We just don't have enough time to do what we think we need to do; we do not even have time to do what we really need to do.

That is time poverty. Just as we have seen with money, with time we are also seeing the loss of values and the loss of the sense of what a human being is all about.

At the same time, as Jacob Needleman showed so beautifully in his book *Money and the Meaning of Life*, there is a requirement to go beyond our outward needs, desires, and struggles to connect with the source levels of our being.[3]

Throughout all great teachings, we find the core teaching being that we humans are two-natured and that we occupy two worlds, the inner and outer worlds, at the same time. And that meaning appears only in the place between the two worlds, in the relationship of the two worlds. At this time in our history, money has appropriated the time and space of one of these fundamental worlds. This does not mean that money is evil; it is just that evil is that which prevents our conscious awareness of both the inner and the outer worlds. Evil is the lack of relationship between higher and lower and between ontological and metaphysical levels in humans and in society.

To be obsessed by money is to live in hell, because then we refuse to, perhaps cannot, participate in the Other World, in the deeper realities of life. Jesus said, "Render unto Caesar that which is Caesar's, and unto God that which is God's."[4] I believe that there is enormous power and truth to be found in that somewhat enigmatic saying, which came about as Jesus examined the face of a coin that held the image of Caesar. Isn't it interesting that the earliest coins, like the one I wear around my neck, bore a religious symbol on one side, and a secular image on the other—God and Caesar—so that coins were intended as a tool, an instrument to facilitate human interactions in the material world, while helping one to remember one's dependence on God? It was therefore a thing of balance between the two worlds and a symbol of the two worlds in the ancient world.

The challenge of human life, then, is to render unto Caesar that which is Caesar's, no more and no less, and unto God that which is God's, no more and no less. It is to live a two-natured life, according to the unique structure of our human nature. Early monastic systems attempted something like this, in which the two natures could take place in the form of work and spiritual pursuits within a community of practice. Unfortunately, these communities often became an escape from everyday life and human nature and, ultimately, even places where money became a means of bribery and corruption.

Protestantism rose at exactly the same time as the growth of cities, the so-called discovery of the so-called New World, and the huge quantities of gold and silver pouring into Europe from the conquered lands. It was inevitable therefore that the Protestant work ethic would eventually influence the worldly materialism of the modern era.

People began to feel themselves as defined by money. Indeed, it turned into the principle means of human exchange in a society that was losing so many of its earlier, fundamental traditions. Money could buy almost anything we could want, but the real problem was that we came to want only the things that money can buy.

We acknowledge that we live in a world which is so monetized that the present mixed reality is one in which the cosmic laws of Nature are in many ways covered over and obscured by the mental technology of finance. And how a person behaves toward money is often the test of their authenticity, even though one's character should be tested by a much broader range of challenges. As Needleman noted, "That money is where most of us are tested says precisely as much about the weakness of man as it does about the power of money."[5] What is secondary in life has taken so much of our attention that it leaves little time and energy left for what is primary. This brings up the issue that too many face of selling out. Needleman reminded us, "It is more and more a source of suffering for modern people who feel they must compromise what they consider sacred or morally obligatory in order to satisfy material needs, and are thus prevented from respecting themselves."[6]

This has resulted in so many people feeling that their way of making money is not honorable and that the psychological stress of their job puts them almost daily into a hell where the reward for the job, especially in office jobs, is "only" money. I can't tell you how many female lawyers under thirty-five years of age I meet who are about to jump ship (if they have not already done so) in order to find more meaningful employment. They have lost the sense of the soul of law. Have you ever felt that you want to switch to some more meaningful work that fulfills some real human need and get paid for it? So to answer the big question, how do we know when we are selling out?

Needleman offered a wonderful response and that is to begin the search for an independent attention in oneself that is not ruled by the ego. That is mindfulness with no frills attached. That means that you truly observe the contradictions and compromises that make up your social self—to see yourself as you are. It is that power that we can respect, and there is probably no better situation for this kind of self-observation than occasions in which money is involved. You can have a feast on all your issues when it involves paying the mortgage or a loan or making monetary decisions. You can even become sincere with yourself. So far from being the instrument of the devil, money serves to give us back ourselves uncensored.

Render unto Caesar the things that are Caesar's—and no more. We are built to occupy the two worlds, the inner and the outer realities simultaneously and, in so doing, build the third world of the human possibility. This third world is the source of our imagination, our creativity, our dignity and, yes, even our true profit. By expanding our engagement with this realm, we bring our growth and our creative expression or accomplishments back and share them as gifts with others, even God or the Universe. Then we know that whenever we have experienced self-serving greed, it really has had its source in the absence of this third world of inner spirit. Greed is ultimately limited when, through the ego, it tends to satisfy itself only through material gains. That is why so many spiritual teachers speak of the breakdown of the ego as a requirement for true growth and meaning.

In the third world, the mind is convinced that the sources of its well-being are expanded states of consciousness. The real work of studying ourselves, painful as that can be—but helped along particularly when it comes to issues of money—is that we are able to discover depths of ourselves that go beyond the one-dimensional focus of personal gain. These are inevitably more universal levels and the higher forces of life. This is the morality of the source, the adventuring into yourself to find the third world of creative potency and possibility where the good of the whole becomes the context for your creativity. New pathways open up as the new ideals and principles are brought back to the outer world for manifestation. Then you are able to work with joy and give much of yourself and your substance, render unto Caesar that which is appropriate, and give the gifts of your being and, yes, the fruits of your labor back into God. As Meister Eckhart said:

> We are not really alive until we have borne the gift back into the Godhead. Whatever has proceeded from the Godhead comes to life, or receives its being, only the moment when it 'gazes back' toward Him. The circuit must be completed. Man ought to be flowing out into whatever can receive him.[7]

This brings up the whole question of worldview. What makes our worldview so fundamental to our existence? It can't be just the huge economic investments that derive from the materialist view. Indeed, the whole materialist marketplace mentality of technology and science as we know it is threatened by a worldview that tells us of vast realms unavailable to our direct observation. In fact, a result of the worldview in which we are embedded is, ultimately, the destruction of the material playground, the earth itself as a living organism.

Annie Leonard's wonderful short film *The Story of Stuff* was first an hour-long talk about how our consumer society began and why we are all so obsessed with being good consumers, buying and hoarding material items that we don't even need and that ultimately won't bring us satisfaction. Annie discovered that our consumer-driven society is in a great deal of trouble. Basically, she said our planet has a finite amount of resources to begin with, and we have a linear system on a finite planet, and we want it to run forever, which of course it can't. Of the one hundred largest economies on earth, fifty-one are corporations, which make them bigger than many governments. These corporations are only interested in profits, so they have to keeping selling stuff to us. The problem is that we're running out of resources. As Annie said, "We are cutting and mining and hauling and trashing the place so fast that we're undermining the planet's very ability for people to live here."[8]

In our consumer-driven society we are asked to buy into the fantasy that we need all sorts of products that in fact have no real meaning in our lives. And what happens once we have purchased all this stuff? An amazing 99 percent of all these goods are thrown away within six months.

Retailing analyst Victor Lebow was quoted as saying:

Our enormously productive economy demands that we make consumption our way of life, that we convert the buying and use of goods into rituals, that we seek our spiritual satisfaction, our ego satisfaction, in consumption. We need things consumed, burned up, replaced and discarded at an ever-accelerating rate.[9]

During Eisenhower's presidency, the chairman of the Council of Economic Advisors, Arthur F. Burns said, "The American economy's ultimate purpose is to produce more consumer goods." Thus the great minds of US government turned us away from spiritual pursuits in favor of buying a never-ending supply of products based on planned obsolescence and perceived obsolescence. Why else would fashions change every three months and computers and cell phones need to be upgraded every year? We are being sold a bill of goods to keep us working until we drop in order to keep us consuming items we don't need. In other words, we are being sold a manufactured reality that clearly does not serve us or the planet.

However, I believe that this governance of ideas has come to its end. With so much information available through the media, the internet, and extensive public education, everybody is getting smart. People know our own experiences and we what they have undergone does not fit the prevailing mechanistic worldview. It is apparent that large percentages of people seem to know there is an unseen world or other dimensions of reality. They may not call it that, but they know that the subtle realms and a larger reality exist. They know their own experiences and trust them. They are not fooled by NBC or the *New York Times* or *Time* magazine or other official arbiters of reality and the truth. We have a kind of revolution going on here, an underground of popular knowledge about the world and the Universe. But this Universe is not the one we are being officially told about. It is really going to be interesting to see when the official mainstream, the small percentage of elites that determines what we are supposed to think is real, wakes up to the fact that the consensus view of reality is gone.

My great friend Margaret Mead once wrote:

People still ask each other, "Do you believe in UFOs?" I think
this is a silly question, born of confusion. Belief has to do with
matters of faith. It has nothing to do with the kind of knowledge
that is based on scientific inquiry . . . When we want to understand something strange, something previously unknown, we
have to begin with an entirely different set of questions. What is
it? How does it work? Are there recurrent regularities?[10]

That quote actually grew out of a discussion between us on the
nature of the phenomenon. Under the influence of Margaret Mead, this
is the way I try to conduct my investigations into who and what we are
and what is happening to reality.

What I discover is that there is another generative possibility that
engages a far more productive and creative worldview than the one we
know, one that not only gives us the keys to the kingdom but the ways
and means to be good and vital stewards of a world in transition. New
Thought minister Mary Morrissey said:

Transformation doesn't necessarily happen overnight. When we
travel down life's highway, we make small shifts. A slight move
today, another shift tomorrow, and in six months' time, we will
find ourselves in a totally new place. We find a new sense of
being right with ourselves and a whole new sense of connection
with God.[11]

We enhance the awareness of the physical body, inside and out, and
the sensory systems as well, seeing them as quite fluid and as primarily
creative, resting and residing in a physical world of continuous creation.

We discover that we have optimal templates for body, mind, and spirit. Some came in with us at birth and some are species derivative. When our lives are informed and graced by the energies of essence, we come to live the larger life we were meant to have. When we are engaged in this larger life, there is no room for entropy.

We know that the mind tends to think most about that to which it is most exposed. As my friend Mary Morrissey said, "Whatever enters the mind repeatedly occupies and shapes the mind, and ultimately, is what we become. The events we attend, the material we read, the music we hear, the conversations we hold, the daydreams we entertain, ultimately determine our destiny."[12] Again, we return to the idea of mirror neurons and how they create the need to surround ourselves with supportive friends and those things that are healthy and uplifting as we make this journey.

I ask you to take on a new discipline, one that gets you to pay attention to your own thought life. Ask yourself: *What am I thinking?* The first step toward transforming thoughts is becoming aware of them. In other words, I want you to place in the center of your consciousness a high witness who can gently say to you, *Is all of this toxic thought helping to advance the world?* I know that this is not easy. It helps if we can remember and refocus on why we chose to wake up and take action in the first place. What called you and ignited your passion? What pulls you in a positive direction?

It is easy to feel overwhelmed, discouraged, and disconnected in these turbulent times, but take some time to shift your attention to those things that bring you joy, feed your heart, and inspire you. One way you can rekindle your passion and refuel your connection to the things that matter most is by feeding yourself good experiences and feelings; pour blessings into the hollow spaces.

Process: Filling the Heart with Gratitude

To do this, sit comfortably with your feet on the floor. Close your eyes and take three deep, easy breaths in through your nose and out through your mouth, focusing on your heart. Feel its rhythmic beat. There is the space within your chest that your physical heart occupies, and there is the space all around you that your spiritual heart occupies. Thank your heart for all of the beautiful work it does every moment to keep you alive.

As you continue to breathe in and out, imagine your heart gently expanding just a little bit. Our hearts hold memories and images, big and small. Think of your favorite spot in nature, a place where you feel strongly connected to the elements. What is around you? Is it warm or cool? Are there trees? Water? In your mind, look all around you; use all of your senses. Imagine this place in all of its expansive grandeur.

Shift in your focus now to one specific detail in the scene. It could be a golden honeybee on a blossom or a tiny curved shell on the beach. Fill your heart with other images from nature that you particularly love. Thank these things for blessing you.

Think now of any animals or live creatures you love or may have loved in the past—the equivalents of Toto for you. Picture them happy and healthy, romping and purring. You might include wild beings you feel drawn to: wolves, ravens, dolphins, or elephants. Imagine their warm fur, their feathers lit by sunshine, their tails splashing the surface of the sea as they dive. Use all of your senses. What do they sound like? Smell like? Feel like? Fill your heart with images of these beloved creatures and thank them for blessing you.

Imagine a Yellow Brick Road that runs from a wonderful place in the distance straight through your heart. All of your favorite people are followed by your ancestors, walking, skipping, and dancing along the road. Gently and easily expand your heart to embrace this parade of friends and family. Expand it enough to embrace the miraculous entirety of each one's life on this earth, all of the pain, all of the glory.

Now expand your heart to include all human beings, those of the past, present, and future: fishermen in France, weavers in Guatemala, doctors in South Africa, scientists in Japan, sheep shearers in New Zealand. People of all ages everywhere. Bless and thank each person as he or she passes through your heart. Imagine this blessing and gratitude lifting them up, filling their hearts.

Imagine your heart expanding to encompass the entire earth. Pour your loving energy into the oceans, mountains, forests, cities, villages, and desserts. Think of all the wonderful things this earth provides for the creatures who live upon her: air, water, shelter, food, and beauty. Bless and thank the earth for all of her love, abundance, and life-sustaining generosity.

Move your heart's awareness out into space to encompass the sun that gives us warmth and light, to the moon and all of the planets. Move out through the solar system into the expanding Universe, now blessed and enhanced by your conscious thoughts and blessings.

Imagine all of the beings on the other side of the veil who care so much about our welfare—the invisible helpers who assist us the moment we ask. Send them gratitude through your heart.

Expand your awareness out to touch upon the very Source of all existence—the life force that keeps it all going. Breathe it in. Pour love and gratitude out as you exhale. Do this several times until your heart feels full.

Slowly and easily pull your consciousness back from the Source, back from the solar system, back from the Earth, back from all of the beings human and otherwise from both sides of the veil, back from your favorite places in the natural world, and finally back into your radiant heart.

Feel the beating of your physical heart once more in the center of your chest. Know that these things you have cherished are always with you.

If you feel moved to do so, you could write a thank-you note to the world for all it has given you. You can also feed your heart by creating a collage of things you love and placing it in a prominent place where you can see it often.

How else could you feed your heart using each of your senses? What could you do with joy that you have never done before but always wished you could?

Once our own hearts have been filled, we have more available to give to others. One gift we can give of ourselves is the gift of radical empathy, affirming the deeper essence of people we meet, strengthening our ability to see some good in everyone—the potential and greater core of each individual. We can choose to love others with the gift of truly seeing them and listening to them, of being fully present with our attention. When we take the time to do this, the "otherness" disappears, and we establish resonance in our relationships.

Everything is connected; our thoughts and actions have consequences. We choose from moment to moment what we allow into our hearts and minds and what we do not. We can see injustice in the world and ignore it with a shrug, or we can expand our compassionate hearts and act.

Realize that if an idea is really important to you or your time, considerable resistance will often arise to impede your commitment to its becoming. We must be strong, reconnect with ourselves and others, recommit to our goals, and resist the urge to give up. We must step into our mythic selves and cocreate within that greater story. We no longer have the luxury of extended periods of entropy.

Perhaps the emerging new Renaissance of spirit is what the Mayans and the Hopi people have prophesized. They have long foretold the end of a World Age and the transition to a new order of being. As the Elders Oraibi of the Hopi Nation told us, "Create your community. Be good to each other. And do not look outside yourself for the leader. We are the ones we've been waiting for."[13]

It is time for us to turn off our televisions and tune in to the Wise One, the Wizard within us who has the power to re-green the world and create a bright future for all beings.

● ● ● ●

With the help of ever-vigilant Glinda, Dorothy and her friends shake off the effects of the poppy field. Although the falling snow briefly causes the Tin Man to rust again, with a little oil in the right places, he is good as new. The four allies and Toto, too, continue through the field, back onto the Yellow Brick Road and into the Emerald City of Oz.

8

A HORSE OF A
DIFFERENT COLOR

After a long and arduous journey through the kaleidoscopic landscape of Oz, and after having conquered the poppy field entropy employed by the Wicked Witch of the West in order to stop them, Dorothy and her allies once again return to the Yellow Brick Road. With renewed enthusiasm, they rush toward the great gates of the shimmering Emerald City rising up before them as clear, sweet voices announce in song that they are "out of the woods."[1]

The Emerald City represents the possible world, the greening that Dorothy needs to bring back with her into bleak, gray Kansas. The entire city appears to be green, a color that represents health, vibrancy, growth, and a verdant environment. It can also symbolically be a color of prosperity. The green, sparkling city inspires a sense of religious grandeur, almost the same feeling of awe that one finds at ancient temples and sacred sites. Characteristic of sacred buildings, it has a series of gates that the travelers must pass through before they can make his or her way into the inner sanctum.

The group marches optimistically up to the enormous city gates and rings the bell. An irritable old gatekeeper answers the door and cries out, "Who rang that bell?" (He is really the Wizard in disguise, but of course our travelers would have no way of knowing this.) The gatekeeper demands to know why the visitors did not read the sign clearly displayed on the door. Upon discovering that there is no sign, he puts one there. The sign reads: BELL OUT OF ORDER, PLEASE KNOCK.

When the friends knock the second time, the fellow answers again and asks them to state their business. Dorothy announces that they want to see the Wizard, whereby they are told, "Nobody can see the Great Oz. Nobody's ever seen the Great Oz. Even I have never seen him!" At first blush, he appears to be merely a confused, befuddled, and eccentric old fellow. In fact, he is a manifestation of all the guardians and gatekeepers to the Deep Mysteries throughout time who appear to challenge one's resolve. Here the allies finally stand on the threshold where all of their dreams may come true only to be turned away. In the great tradition of the Hero's Journey, our friends are barred at the gate, their hopes dashed at the very moment of triumph.

"I've got to see the Wizard," Dorothy declares. "The Good Witch of the North sent me!" When asked to prove it, Dorothy shows the Doorman the magical ruby slippers glittering on her feet, whereby he grants them entry into what can only be described as the Utopian Society. Once inside the gates of this art deco citadel of wonders, they are greeted with joy, laughter, singing, and celebrating as the citizens busily bustle about their business.

A friendly carriage driver offers the four friends and Toto a ride, and they accept. (Had they not been distracted by the overwhelming excitement offered by the city, they may have noticed that the carriage driver is none other than our Wizard, in disguise once again. One wonders if he dons these various guises in order to keep a vigilant eye on the various activities taking place within the city without being recognized.) The marvelous carriage is drawn by the famous Horse of a Different Color—a magical beast that changes colors from moment to moment as they clop merrily through the streets. Our heroes are exposed to new sights at every turn.

In the book *The Wonderful Wizard of Oz*, L. Frank Baum told us that the people of the Emerald City all wear green-tinted glasses so that everything they gaze upon is rich with green imagery. What would that be like? Imagine looking through green-tinted lenses and seeing everything as green: glorious green for healing and health; green for growing; green for the heart of a nurturing, possible world pulsing with life, *prana*. The city itself is not just green but emerald, that rare stone of luscious, rich, liquid-deep green, colored by trace amounts of chromium and vanadium.

The Emerald City is quite literally a jewel kingdom that honors and celebrates diversity in its citizens. We have proof of this when we observe that not one citizen is thrown for even a second at the sudden entrance of a human child and her dog, a lion, a scarecrow, and a man made entirely of tin strolling through the courtyard together. Everyone warmly welcomes the members of the eclectic group, without question.

Within this glowing jewel, we find lavish expressions of art deco architecture, creativity, and fun. Each of the citizens wears a green costume, symbolizing the group's shared vision of the Emerald City, its beliefs and constructs. Here we would most likely find teaching and learning communities and active Social Artists all content to make things happen while supporting one another. A well-rounded education for all people that includes rich cultivation of the imagination and the arts would be considered critical for the society to survive and thrive. In her book *The Road to Oz*, author Kathleen Krull quoted L. Frank Baum as having once written that he wanted his stories to inspire day-dreams in children because: "the imaginative child will become the imaginative man or woman most able to create, to invent, and therefore to foster civilization."[2] Infused with this creative imagination as a society, the people of the Emerald City are able to explore life's possibilities beyond the box of what has been done before. Albert Einstein once said that "no problem can be solved from the same level of consciousness that created it."[3] Rather than being relegated to the back- seat of education, if acknowledged at all, the role of the imagina-tion must therefore be cultivated and valued in this new world we are creating.

What are some of the other unseen components that might make this society so successful? As our allies glide along in their carriage, we can see that the streets of the Emerald City are very clean. Perhaps the citizens are skilled and innovative with their use of the material waste that is gener-ated. Rather than filling up toxic dumps, they recycle as much as they can, consistently discovering new uses for the recycled products.

We can imagine such a place relying on biomimicry (from the Greek *bios*, meaning "life," and *mimesis*, meaning "to imitate"), where one observes the ways in which Nature deals with problems and copies those solutions, successfully adapting them to human needs. Velcro is a good example of biomimicry being used to create something useful. Its inventor, a Swiss gentleman named George de Mestral, came up with the idea in 1948 after closely observing the burrs that stuck tenaciously to his dog's fur. Using a microscope, he noticed tiny hooks on the end of the burr spines that caught onto clothing, hair, and fur. Though many people did not take his idea seriously at first, the inventor confidently believed that his invention would be as effective and popular as the zipper, which it proved to be.[4]

Another innovative example of biomimicry in action can be found in the designs of the Prince Claus Award–winning green architect Mick Pearce, who studied how termites in Zimbabwe kept their towerlike mounds at a comfortable and constant internal temperature through the use of passive cooling. Pearce noticed that as temperatures in the region fluctuated from 35 degrees Fahrenheit at night to 104 degrees Fahrenheit during the day, the termites dug breeze-catchers at the base of their mounds, which cooled the air by means of chambers carved out of the wet mud below and sent hot air out through a flue to the top. They constantly varied this construction by alternatively opening up new tunnels and blocking others to regulate the heat and humidity within the mound. (Termites die when the temperature rises above 33 degrees Fahrenheit.)

Pearce has built many amazing buildings in Africa using this principle of passive cooling. Perhaps best known is his enormous Eastgate Centre building in Harare, designed to mimic those tower-building termites. The building uses no air conditioners. "Eastgate is the country's largest office and shopping complex and expends less than 10 percent of the energy used in similar sized conventional high rises."[5]

Mick Pearce's most recent work involves developing passive control systems in small-scale single-story buildings as well as large-scale multistory buildings using methods that rely even less on imported materials, technologies, or human resources.

In their book *Cradle To Cradle*, William McDonough and Michael Braungart argued that the conflict between industry and the environment is an outgrowth of purely opportunistic design. Today, however, with our knowledge of the living earth, design can reflect a new spirit. McDonough's design paradigm suggests that designers employ the intelligence of natural systems such as the effectiveness of nutrient cycling, the abundance of the sun's energy, and so forth, to create products, industrial systems, buildings, and even regional plans that allow nature and commerce to fruitfully coexist.[6] Imagine this blend of nature and green technology with beautiful design being used everywhere in the Emerald City.

Many cities around the world are waking up to the benefits of bringing more of the natural environment into urban communities in the form of rooftop gardens. Rooftops heat up under the sun's rays, increasing the air temperature, thus heating up the occupied space below. Some rooftops are now being covered with vegetation to counteract this effect. Germany has been a leader in green-roof technology for over three decades. In this densely populated and developed country that struggles with annual river floods, a green roof can also help to alleviate storm water runoff. The country has over 100 million square feet of green rooftops that absorb rainwater and restore the natural hydrologic processes. Living roofs also help to insulate homes.

Studies on green roofs atop Chicago's big buildings reveal that those structures can expect a 10 percent reduction in air-conditioning costs. In other studies, scientists have found that green roofs on smaller buildings can reduce solar heat gain by 95 percent and reduce cooling needs from 25 to 50 percent.[7]

Just imagine how literally everything in our lives would be changed if we learned from Nature and worked with her rather than dominated it. This would include not only our food production but the ways in which we gather and use energy, make materials, heal ourselves, store information, conduct business, run governance, and discover the mysteries behind who and what we really are and what our purpose on Earth is at this time.

The most important thing to know is that Nature by its very nature is imaginative! And by order of its enormously imaginative powers, it has solved all of the problems that we are currently struggling with. As Janine Benyus wrote in *Biomimicry: Innovation Inspired by Nature*:

When we stare deeply into nature's eyes, it takes our breath away, and in a good way, it bursts our bubble. We realize that all our inventions have already appeared in nature in a more elegant way and at a lot less cost to the planet. Our most clever architectural struts and beams are already featured in lily pads and bamboo stems. Our central heating and air-conditioning are bested by the termite tower's steady 86 degrees F. Our most stealthy radar is hard of hearing compared to a bat's multi-frequency transmission. And our new "smart materials" can't hold a candle to the dolphin's skin or the butterfly's proboscis. Even the wheel which we took to be a uniquely human creation has been found in the tiny rotary motor that propels the flagellum of the world's most ancient bacteria.

Humbling also are the hordes of organisms casually performing feats we can only dream about. Bioluminescent algae splash chemicals together to light their body lanterns. Arctic fish and frogs freeze solid and then spring to life, having protected their organs from ice damage. Black bears hibernate all winter without poisoning themselves on their urea, while their polar cousins stay active, with a coat of transparent hollow hairs covering their skins like the panes of a greenhouse. Chameleons and cuttlefish hide without moving, changing the pattern of their skin to instantly blend in with their surroundings. Bees, turtles, and birds navigate without maps, while whales and penguins dive without scuba gear. How do they do it? How do dragonflies outmaneuver our best helicopters? How do hummingbirds cross the Gulf of Mexico on less than one tenth of an ounce of fuel? How do ants carry the equivalent of hundreds of pounds in a dead heat through the jungle?

These individual achievements pale, however, when we consider the intricate inter-living that characterizes whole systems, communities like tidal marshes or Saguaro forests. In ensemble, living things maintain a dynamic stability, like dancers in an arabesque, continually juggling resources without waste.[8]

What would our political, social, and personal lives be like if we could learn the dynamics of whole-system interliving that characterizes communities in Nature? Nature is an inspired psychologist and a brilliant Social Artist to boot. For if we look at Nature's laws, strategies, and principles, we discover that:

Nature runs on sunlight.
Nature uses only the energy it needs.
Nature fits form to function.
Nature recycles everything.
Nature rewards cooperation.
Nature banks on diversity.
Nature demands local expertise.
Nature curbs excesses from within.
Nature taps the power of limits.

When we look through our green lens in the Emerald City, we see all of these amazing possibilities abounding. What else do we see through our green glasses? There are no homeless people in the

Emerald City. There is no poverty, no hunger. All of the citizens are clean, well-fed, and happy. How was all of this accomplished?

Process: The Emerald City/One World Over

I believe that we can learn how to solve many of the problems facing our society today by looking at how they may have been solved in the Emerald City. I want you to imagine that the people of Oz might have gotten themselves into some of the same quandaries that we find ourselves in today. Perhaps Oz went through an industrial age once upon a time, and the Emerald City was filled with smoke and soot. Perhaps there was a time when many people found themselves out of work and homeless. You get the idea. Somehow, the creative, brilliant people of the Emerald City found solutions to their most perplexing problems. I suggest that we use a process by which we ask them exactly how they did it.

I want you to imagine that the dimension of Oz is simply one world over from our own, that Oz is separated from our own world only by the thinnest of veils. You reach a person who lives in the Emerald City, perhaps the great Wizard of Oz himself, and he tells you, "As we are adjacent to you on the dimensional span, we are closer to you in realities."

You actually get a download of information from the Emerald City to answer how they were able to solve some of their social ills. Pick a topic: environment/ecology, government, education—you name the issue, and we are going to discover how they solved these problems in Oz.

First, sit comfortably with your feet on the floor and breathe slowly and deeply several times, in through the nose and out through the mouth. Relax your body. Fill your heart with the capacity of caring. Ask to receive clear information. What current situation tears at your heart? Ask the question you wish to have answered and imagine that the area where you are sitting is filled with a sacred void, a place that is empty and that is prepared to be filled. Imagine that you put on your green glasses and that you are entering the great gates of the splendid Emerald City itself. Because they care, beings from that city want to come, want to help us. Call upon the wisdom of the people of the Emerald City. They are coming forward to help you now.

Dive through that void, knowing yourself safely anchored and held on a line that will take you to that Other World and also bring you back again. Let it happen now.

Dive. Pull. Be there. In Oz. In the Emerald City.

Use all of your senses. See it. Feel the breeze of Oz. Smell the poppy fields.

You are there now.

You see someone wearing green coming toward you, coming to greet you. You are led, you are guided, and you are shown the ways that this society got beyond its problems and flourished. You are being shown solutions to the things that matter the most to you. You are being told how it happened, how they got out of the quandary, how they improved and enhanced their society. See the solutions; feel them; hear them. Use all of your senses to take in this vital, very specific information that you can bring back to change our own world.

Connect once again to the issue about which you care most deeply. Thank your friend in Oz for this gift and guidance. As the download of solutions is complete, release the Emerald City and dive back into our own world. Return with great gratitude.

Be here now, filled with solutions from the Emerald City. What have you brought back with you? You may wish to take some time to write down or draw pictures of everything you saw and heard there.

Know that you can return to the Emerald City any time you wish to gain insight, to bring back to our world knowledge, to bring back future stories of Oz and the happy citizens of the possible world.

Checking in on Dorothy and her companions once again, one of the first things that you notice is jolly music, followed by laughter. As they work, the citizens sing a catchy song called "The Merry Old Land of Oz" (lyrics by E. Y. Harburg). The song is chock-full of laughter and happy sounds of Nature.

Now, how can a person possibly have a bad day when submerged in the power of laughter such as our friends find themselves in the Emerald City? There is an old Apache tale that I remember from my teens that spoke of the Creator making man able to do everything— talk, run, look, and hear. But the Creator wasn't quite satisfied with his work. He wanted man to be able to do just one more thing, and that was laugh. And upon this last act by the Creator, man laughed and laughed and laughed. And the Creator said, "Now you are fit to live."

Arthur Schopenhauer once said that "a sense of humor is the only divine quality of man."[9] That was, by the way, one of Carl Jung's favorite quotes. Indeed, it would seem that the more we laugh, the closer we are to the God World from whence we came. As newborns, we discover that this planet is a funny place, and upon closer examination of wiggling fingers and toes, one's body is the funniest of all. By ten months old, the baby finds visual things funny, such as faces, especially parents making deliberately comical actions. And what we grown-ups won't do to get that smile or chuckle. We get on our hands and knees and turn our faces into pulled taffy—all for that divine look of God giggling at us through the baby.

When babies are about a year old, they begin to become conscious comedians themselves, instigating peek-a-boo and games of hide-and-seek, or they pretend to fall down accidentally. Banana-peel pratfall humor begins at this age. By the time children turn four or five years old, they are particularly turned on by slapstick, laughing on average about once every four minutes.

It is a strange and lamented fact that as we get older we laugh less. This is really unfortunate. Much has been written about the power of laughter's ability to heal, uplift our spirits, fill us with joy, and help keep our lives in perspective.[10] Indeed, the Old Testament told us in Proverbs 17:22: "A merry heart doeth good like a medicine."

Various studies have shown that humor and laughter help people live longer, happier lives; be more creative and productive; and have more energy with less physical discomfort.[11] As we all know, humor reduces stress, fear, intimidation, and anger.[12] Laughter may also have extraordinary healing power.[13] When a person laughs, blood pressure decreases, heart rate and respiration increase, the body releases endorphins, and depression declines.[14] After the laughter subsides and you relax again, that good feeling has a lasting effect, even until the next day.[15]

Imagine what the power of laughter can do for a society and the green world we are creating. I can speak from personal experience about this topic since my father, Jack Houston, was a professional comedian and one of the writers of *The Bob Hope Show*. Laughing through the smoke-filled rooms of our bungalow, I remember my dad working with his fellow comedy writers. As their talk with each other was all by means of punch lines, I never quite understood what they were saying, but I laughed anyway.

The preschool kids in the neighborhood came to join me in these afternoon sessions. I have recently recovered a memory of a line of us like some kids out of the *Our Gang* comedy show—the girls bedecked with Shirley Temple curls and bows, the boys with scabby knees and baseball caps too big for them—all sitting to one side, also not understanding the conversation-by-punch-line but laughing uproariously all the same. Why did they come day after day? Because they liked to laugh. It's what children do. While I tried to write my autobiography at one time, these memories caused me some consternation because as I reviewed my early childhood, all that came out of it was comedy. A friend of mine who is oriented to the Jungian point of view once advised me to part the curtains on the scenes or open the door into another room beyond the laughter so as to find, she assured me, the shadows that would be hidden there. I did as she suggested. I opened the door and found myself in the kitchen where my mother was listening in and laughing.

I have read many, many definitions and disquisition on comedy and humor. I've followed its tracks in the Middle Ages and the Renaissance, where humor meant one of the four principle body fluids that determine human dispositions and health (sanguine, phlegmatic, choleric, melancholic). And in physiology it still refers to body fluids. The secondary definitions in dictionaries also look back to the Renaissance and define *humor* as a state of mind and spirit. The root of the word is the Latin *umor*, meaning "liquid, fluid." Humor, therefore, as Helen Luke reminded us, is on all levels:

> Something that flows, resembling water itself, and symbolizes the movement of the unconscious forces gradually evolving into basic characteristics of the individual human being, which expresses themselves in the body, in moods, and in emotional reactions, in qualities of feeling, of mind, and of spirit.[16]

Our humors, therefore, are our unconscious drives and reactions, the things boiling up in our reality from beneath the surface crust of consciousness. The sense of humor is the capacity to appreciate and understand this boiling as it emerges into life and time.

Taking these factors into consideration, I would like to give you my definition: Comedy and humor are, at their best, the discovery of the unexpected universe both within and without ourselves and then the cockeyed reinvention of that universe. It's a God job rendered hilarious. And maybe it's God's job after all. *Putting together the unlikely and the improbable from the unseen to create the unusual for the unprepared.* This is the manner of creation! This is the stuff of evolution! This is the laughter at the heart of things! I have seen too many sight gags in nature not to believe that some stupendous sense of humor wasn't behind it all. Just watch a sloth climb a tree, for instance. Or a duck following a billiard ball it thinks is his mama. Watch a geyser like Old Faithful burble and giggle, and then burst into life. Superheated water eruption? Nonsense. Somebody or something just told it a joke.

Also take note of people whose minds and thoughts are given to a comically appreciative point of view. Almost invariably they have many more comical episodes in their lives than do others with a more serious view of things. Nature and fate conspire to give these people a humorous universe. Now you may say that really it is only their capacity to appreciate the humor of life situations, or to note the nature of the absurd in the ordinary, but I say it is more. Having grown up with an authentically funny man, I would have to conclude that something mysterious was always afoot.

In the humorous universe, there is a great deal more experience to be had; one lives more life, sees more sides, and then goes back to invent the world in which these added sides and scenes are part of the extraordinary ordinary. How do you do this? Freedom produces jokes, and jokes produce freedom. Through playing with the ideas that occur in jokes, the universe of ideas is greatly extended. Think for a moment about the least empowering moments in your life. Is there a way you could transform them with good humor into laughter? Consider the tragic flaws, the pressures of time and space, the fall of the noble into dust and anguish, the audience's experience of empathy—pity and terror. Comedy is exactly the same thing, except that the audience laughs and releases energy.

Here arc some techniques that we can use to transform incidents into humor:

Exaggeration
Turning things upside down
Looking for puns or possible wordplay
Deliberately transgressing further across the boundary
Inviting the action of oneself as Fool, observing oneself
Using many subpersonalities to comment upon or analyze the
    situation
Asking foolish questions
Using analogy (instead of people doing the actions, it might be
    frogs or birds)

Laughter is good for you. It causes you to take in more oxygen, thus to be "inspirited." It increases your metabolism by stirring up the endocrine system; it exercises the diaphragm and stomach muscles, in addition to massaging the internal organs. It grows new dendrites in the brain and offers insights into hidden places. It turns your personality and subpersonalities into rubber! And it helps to release us into the higher purposes of our lives. Comedy keeps our hearts light, our bodies healthy, and our spirits refreshed. So, I urge you to take the time to check out a book of jokes from the library, spend an evening watching comedy DVDs, enjoy funny stories, and find the humor of this planet—so rich in material—on which we find ourselves.

Amid gales of laughter, our heroes are taken to the Emerald City Wash and Brush Up Shop—a first-rate spa—where they are washed, pressed, combed, coiffed, ironed, and fluffed in order to see the Wizard. Each worker sings happily and seems to take pride in his or her work. In fact, their activities seem more like fun than work, as each person is doing the job he or she has felt called to do. It does not appear as if some members of the city are thought of more highly than others. All work is honored, serves a purpose, and contributes to the good of the whole, and they are having fun doing it.

In his book *A Whole New Mind*, Daniel H. Pink provided us with an example of an older way of thinking where work and play (or fun) did not mix. At the Ford Motor Company's Rogue River plant in the 1930s and 1940s "laughter was a disciplinary offense—and humming, whistling, and smiling were evidence of insubordination."[17] In his book, Pink quoted British management scholar David Collinson's story:

> In 1940 John Gallo was sacked because he was "caught in the act of smiling" after having committed an earlier breach of "laughing with the other fellows and slowing down the line maybe half a minute." This tight managerial discipline reflected the overall philosophy of Henry Ford, who stated that "When we are at work we ought to be at work. When we are at play we ought to be at play. There is no use trying to mix the two."[18]

Pink asserted that modern businesses have found that, in fact, mixing work and play has improved business. He cited Southwest Airlines, one of the leading carriers in the United States, a company that "earns regular profits while its competitors wobble on the edge of solvency." Reading through the airline's mission statement that says, in part, "people rarely succeed at anything unless they are having fun doing it," we get a glimpse of the attitude that is key to the company's success. The flight attendants, wearing shorts, polo shirts and tennis shoes rather than the dark polyester business suits required by other airlines, are encouraged to be relaxed and joke with passengers while at the same time performing all of their professional safety duties seriously. Passengers have responded favorably to this combination of professionalism and fun, and they return to the carrier again and again when making their travel plans. This is not the only business to bring fun into the workplace. More and more businesses (especially in Europe) are discovering its value.

Pink went on to say:

Humor is showing itself to be an accurate marker for managerial effectiveness, emotional intelligence, and the thinking style characteristic of the brain's right hemisphere. And joyfulness, as exemplified by unconditional laughter, is demonstrating its power to make us more productive and fulfilled.[19]

Pink concluded his chapter by saying that "plain laughter can lead to joyfulness, which can in turn lead to greater creativity, productivity, and collaboration."[20] The citizens of the Emerald City certainly have figured this out.

The clean-up ritual in which Dorothy and her friends happily partake is similar to those of initiates who must be cleansed and purified before approaching the Holy One or an initiation. It is at this point in the journey that one enters soiled, tired, and bereft of spirit and emerges fresh, clean, and empowered. Here is another example of a society that takes care of its people's personal needs. The newcomers need help? They are helped without question. One can imagine that in the Emerald City, healthcare and childcare are not societal problems. All are treated holistically and with respect. Healthcare for all citizens is taken for granted, and all can go about doing their work with whole and healthy bodies. minds, and spirits.

While working in Java, I met with a shaman who told me that people would feel much better and be healthier if they shook their entire bodies for several minutes every day. Try this. Imagine that you are in the Emerald City Wash and Brush Up Shop. Stand up right now and gently shake, shake, shake your body as if you were being washed and brushed and buffed by magical cleansers. Does your body feel refreshed?

Process: A Three-Minute Vacation

Now we give your mind and spirit some internal refreshment with a three-minute vacation (equal to all the time you need). Sit comfortably in a chair with your feet on the floor. Close your eyes and take three easy, deep breaths in through your nose and out through your mouth. Picture your favorite vacation spot. Bring in all of your senses: smell it, hear the sounds, touch it, taste your favorite foods there. Be specific! Really immerse yourself in this place. Feel all of your cares and worries evaporating. What activities would you like to experience while you're there?

Shift your attention to the next place you would like to visit on this vacation. Are you camping in a tent or are you in a fine hotel room? What is all around you? Do you hear crickets chirping or the sounds of bustling traffic outside your window? Are you inhaling pine-scented air or the aroma of a delicious chicken curry offered by a busy street vendor? What will you do for entertainment? Ride your bike? Attend an opera premiere? Remember that you are not restrained by time or space. Feel free to explore the best vacation spots of ancient Greece or the summer palace of the emperor of China. When you have experienced one place to your satisfaction, move on to the next and the next until your three minutes are up. Come back into your room, fully relaxed.

So let us return to a refreshed young Dorothy now in an immaculately pressed gingham dress, her hair scented and braided, her cheeks rosy. The Cowardly Lion is clean and curled, a bright bow in his shining fur; the Scarecrow is very dapper, having been stuffed with fresh straw; and the Tin Man has been well-oiled and buffed until he gleams with splendor. Even Toto is spotless and ready to meet the great Wizard.

Chaos, however, encroaches on the friends' fun and excitement once again in the form of the Wicked Witch of the West, who rides across the sky on her broomstick, spelling out dangerous words formed by noxious gases. The death threat reads:

S-U-R-R-E-N-D-E-R D-O-R-O-T-H-Y.

This represents that moment in any quest where the hero contemplates surrendering herself to the Greater Forces that threaten. Our friends find that the witch's message merely strengthens their resolve. Not knowing who Dorothy is, the concerned citizens of the city race toward the castle, clambering to ask the Wizard within what the omen means, but they are turned away by a guard—(the Wizard himself, in disguise yet again)—who proclaims that everything is all right, the Wizard has everything under control. When Dorothy and her friends tell the gatekeeper that they want to see the Wizard, he says they can't: "Nobody has seen the Great Oz, not nobody, no how."

The Scarecrow insists, "But she is Dorothy." At that point, the guard reconsiders and declares that he will ask the Wizard if an audience might be granted. In the few hopeful minutes that follow, the Cowardly Lion imagines the Wizard granting his wish for courage. Draped in a makeshift king's robe and broken pottery crown, he sings one of the most memorable songs in movie history, "If I Were King of the Forest." In the finale he explains: "What makes a king out of a slave? Courage!"

After this proud anthem, the guard returns and promptly tells our heroes, "The Wizard says go away!" and he slams the door. They have come a long way and been denied entrance into the very place that is their hearts' dearest desire. Dorothy looks up at the barred threshold, fearing that she will never get back to Kansas. Missing her Auntie Em, she begins to cry, "Auntie Em was so good to me. And I never appreciated it. Running away and hurting her feelings. Professor Marvel said she was sick. She may be dying and it's all my fault. I'll never forgive myself! Never, never, never."

The guard overhears the girl's sorrow and his heart softens. Torrents of tears spring from his eyes and run down his cheeks. He relents and lets them all in, muttering, "I had an Auntie Em myself, once."

The four friends walk down a long, dark hall with many stained-glass windows, a place like the great cathedrals of Europe. With fear and trembling, they approach a massive arched doorway. Knees knocking, they enter at last into the echo-filled reception room of the Great and Terrible Wizard of Oz.

9

WHEN FLYING MONKEYS SWOOP IN

Alarge, luminous head rises up before our heroes amid clouds of smoke and intermittent blasts of fire. The head frowns slightly as the friends approach. This is the Wizard, a seemingly divine being who speaks in the booming, echoing voice of the gods. "Come forward!" the disembodied head commands. All around the explosive Wizard there are the images of the sacred: an altar, candles or incense burners, and what seem to be organ pipes behind him. What had been merely good-humored humbug articles in Professor Marvel's wagon in Kansas, here have become a full revelation of the sacred.

Each of the four companions sees something fearful in the Wizard that relates to him or her. The Scarecrow sees the balls of fire that accompany the booming voice, which could literally turn him to ash. The Tin Man sees the lack of compassion. The Cowardly Lion, who is frightened at the drop of a hat, sees a terrifying being who could totally consume him with its power. Dorothy sees the stern, humorless authority and rigidity she so feared back in Kansas.

They all approach the Wizard with fear and trembling. In a voice like thunder the scowling head proclaims, "I am Oz, the Great and Powerful! Who are YOU?"

Dorothy answers the divine creature in a tiny voice, denying her own power. "I am Dorothy, the Small and Meek. We have come to ask you—"

"Silence!" bellows the head. "The Great and Powerful Oz knows why you have come. Step forward!"

When each member of the group asks the rumbling being for his assistance, the Wizard is truculent and uncompromising. He agrees to grant their requests if they perform for him what he calls a small task: "Bring me the broomstick of the Wicked Witch of the West." In fact, it is no small task. It is a task for Hercules and other mythic heroes. They all realize that in order to accomplish it, they will have to kill the witch. Nevertheless, if they are to receive their gifts, they must do as the Wizard asks. As part of the initiation process of the Hero's Journey, this point is known as Atonement with the Father, for this is where the hero must confront and be initiated by whatever holds power over his or her life. (Years ago, I had a discussion with Joseph Campbell as to whether we could look at *atonement* in a different way: *at-one-ment* that is a higher order of reconciliation. He did not disagree and urged me to continue with this exploration. This is what we are doing here when we understand the seemly contradictory powers of our own nature.) A father figure takes this role in many myths (but in other cases this figure is not necessarily masculine), but in Oz, it is the Wizard himself who holds this role for Dorothy and her allies. They are challenged by him to move beyond the perceived boundaries they have created for themselves. The Wizard demands that they perform a task that proves their true worth. It is the ultimate task that will ultimately enable the allies to gain what they need for themselves and for society. Remember that in any myth we are actually all of the characters. The Wizard is us. We are orchestrating the challenging situations that prod us to rise to our highest potential so we can become who and what we really are. The Wizard not only calls us forth but he has called forth the journey itself.

For you, the challenge here is to discover the task that you never believed you could do, but the Wizard of the inner sanctum of yourself always knew you could, and if you do it, it will change the nature of your belief about yourself. Each of us has a task that we think might be impossible to accomplish, and most of us have done things that we thought were impossible, witch's broomsticks notwithstanding. Your inner Wizard (who, by the way, is another aspect of the Great Friend) stands before you and asks you to recall for a moment the "impossible" things you have done.

And now the Friend Wizard asks you to consider what "impossible" thing you have yet to do in the near future. The Friend Wizard also asks you to vividly imagine yourself actually doing it, with all the difficulties and acts of courage that it may require. Remember that you have allies, a Protector and the Friend to help and accompany you in this task.

We can help ourselves by reframing the traditional Road of Trials that every hero must endure in the Hero's Journey by turning it into a Road of Adventures filled with opportunities for growth, rather than attacks from outside of ourselves. We are not victims. Adversity is not something that a superior, cruel, unseen force is doing to us for kicks. We are active cocreators in our life experiences. Unfortunate pitfalls or misplaced steps along our own Yellow Brick Road are in fact opportunities to learn who we really are and what we are capable of. No matter what adventures (good or ill) we encounter on our journeys, all have been divinely orchestrated by us in order to assist us in our growth as human beings on Earth and our expansion as souls. We learn through experience, not theory alone.

And we learn while in the physical form, so the fact that you now have a body in which to work and learn and grow is really a blessing. As my good friend Pierre Teilhard de Chardin is often quoted as saying, "We are not human beings having a spiritual experience. We are spiritual beings having a human experience."[1]

Process: Your Yellow Brick Road

I'd like you to take out a piece of paper and draw a Yellow Brick Road on it. It doesn't have to be straight; roads rarely are. Add dips and curves as you feel they are appropriate. At one end of the road, place a big dot that represents the beginning of your life's journey, which started with your birth. At the other end of the road, place another big dot that represents the place where you are right now.

Think back on all of the challenging bumps you have had in your life thus far—events or circumstances where you felt particularly sad or angry about what happened to you. Place a dot on the road to represent each of these times. Above each dot briefly write in the circumstance of your bumps in the road as well as the allies that helped you. Interestingly, we often find that people we thought were our enemies at the time were actually our greatest allies in that we would not have evolved to be the people we are now without their prodding us into places we didn't want to go.

Next, imagine that you are your own entelechy. Step into the part of you that is guiding your journey from a higher perspective, as Glinda is guiding Dorothy safely through the Land of Oz. From this wide perspective, looking at your journey in its entirety so far, can you see reasons why those stumbling blocks may have been put in your path? Did you learn anything by going through that situation? Are you a kinder, more compassionate person now than you were before? Have you learned to set more effective boundaries for yourself? Have you honed your pluck and cunning? Did the experience force you to turn inward for answers?

Once Dorothy, Toto, and her allies leave the Emerald City to get the witch's broomstick, they enter into that most dangerous yet exciting part of their journey. Where there was a well-defined Yellow Brick Road to get to the Wizard, there is no clear-cut road to get to the shadow world. Here our friends have been given a task to perform, and they must go through a series of ordeals to test their mettle.

In the dark and twisted wood where the witch's castle lies, the Yellow Brick Road has dissolved. Our heroes are now on the pathless path. In some ways, the haunted forest in the Land of Oz is the parallel image of bleak Kansas. There is no clear way to move about in this shadowland, to get to the task ahead. Perhaps because the task to be done must be carried out in the gray world or the shadow world of limiting thoughts and potentials, social injustice often finds you before you can find it. Time and again in life you are warned, "I'd turn back if I were you." How often have you been told that when you wanted to go out and do something to make the world a better place?

The friends enter the haunted forest loaded with items they hope will help them achieve their objective: a giant can of bug spray and an oversize butterfly net. We know this place is haunted because a weathered sign clearly states HAUNTED FOREST, WITCHES CASTLE, 1 MILE. The Scarecrow reads the posted warnings and proclaims that he does not believe in ghosts, but at that very moment the Tin Man is suddenly lifted high into the air by invisible spirits and is dropped with a terrible, tin-crunching crash to the ground. The Cowardly Lion cringes, wrings his own tail and shuts his eyes, chanting in almost prayerful tones, "I do believe in spooks! I do! I do!"

At that moment an eerie, high-pitched sound like a swarm of locusts (but more menacing) is heard from the sky. From the towers of her castle, the Wicked Witch has sent her dark messengers—flying monkeys—to attack the companions as they make their way through the haunted forest. The soaring beasts fill the air like lethal fighter planes, zeroing in on their prey below. Looking a great deal like flying bats in bellman uniforms when seen close up, the winged monkeys swiftly descend in a cloud of ill omen to terrorize the travelers and create chaos.

Perhaps each of these winged monkeys represents the things in our lives that keep us from moving forward and getting things done. The monkey mind fills our thoughts with ceaseless chatter, fouling our plans of meditation. Our thoughts twist and churn, spinning out of control with our everyday obligations such as going to work, cooking meals, doing laundry, running errands.

Or it may seem to some as though adversity is attacking at every turn. A job may have ended or a relationship terminated. Sometimes it seems as if our lives have tipped completely upside down on the Road of Adventures, and we can't figure out why. Too much! Too much!

Winged monkeys can appear in your life as stress in all of its guises, sometimes becoming so overwhelming that it turns into depression and despair. We may feel swept away from our greater goals, carried to a place that seems utterly hopeless.

The flying beasts capture Dorothy and Toto, lifting them up and carrying them off through the skies toward the castle, leaving the straw man shredded and scattered. This would certainly be one of the Scarecrow's greatest fears realized. Ripped asunder, he is revealed to have little substance. He is only straw mixed with a fierce determination to see Dorothy through to the end.

How many times have you felt torn apart by events in your life? In many cultures and lands, the shamanic journey includes the complete destruction of the dream body as seen in dreams, visions, or trances. Once ceremoniously dismantled, torn apart or, in some cases, eaten, an entirely new body emerges, representing the spiritual identity of the shaman and his or her rebirth into the depth worlds to become the Master of Two Worlds. Just so, the Scarecrow is torn to pieces and must be reassembled by the Tin Man and Lion.

"What happened to you?" the Tin Man queries, looking at the tossed and tangled remains of his companion.

"They took my legs off and they threw them over there!" the Scarecrow bellows. "Then they took my chest out and they threw it over there!"

The Tin Man shakes his head. "Well, that's you all over."

But the steadfast friend of straw is undaunted, saying, "Don't just stand there talking! Put me together! We've got to find Dorothy!" Now that's determination and loyalty.

The Wicked Witch has locked Dorothy in her dark Gothic castle, a fortress akin in grandeur to the Emerald City, set high atop a mountain. (It is, however, seen only at night when shadows haunt the living, in contrast to the Emerald City, which is seen in the full light of day when consciousness reigns.) Magical fire appears in both castles, but instead of inspiring awe and a sense of the sacred as it does in the Emerald City, here it provokes terror by suggesting a very nasty presence lurking in the shadows.

Like the Emerald City, the great stone castle possesses heavily guarded gates and doors. Whereas the entrance to the Emerald City has a benign gatekeeper, the witch's stronghold is surrounded by menacing guards carrying formidable-looking weapons. Unlike the happy and carefree citizens of the Emerald City who intone merry songs, these dreadful creatures march to chants of heavy labor. Some experts on Oz trivia have speculated that the witch's guards are booming, "Oh we loathe the Old One."

The witch, who herself embodies sulfur, flame, and orange smoke, has a diabolic appearance as she sits in her high conjuring tower, stroking a trembling Toto with a green bony hand. "What a nice little dog," she purrs. "And you, my dear. What an unexpected pleasure. It's so kind of you to visit me in my loneliness." At this, the witch places Toto in a basket and hands him to Nikko, the leader of the winged monkeys.

"What are you going to do with my dog?" Dorothy frets. "Give him back to me!"

The witch agrees to give the girl her dog back only when she surrenders the magical ruby slippers. Dorothy consents, but when the witch reaches down to steal the slippers, sparks shoot out and zap her, burning her hands.

"I should have remembered," the Wicked Witch shrieks, recoiling. "Those slippers will never come off as long as you're alive."

At this, faithful Toto (always pushing our story along) leaps from the basket and darts off down dark stairwells and hallways. "Run, Toto, run!" Dorothy cries. And run he does, straight up and over a closing drawbridge and out of the castle to find Dorothy's allies as fast as his little legs can carry him.

Now the infuriated witch has had enough. She turns an ornate hourglass on end and points to the rapidly dripping blood-red sands. "That's how long you've got to be alive." She sneers. "And it isn't long, my pretty. It isn't long!" She leaves poor Dorothy alone in the cold tower, time and life running out. The dream of an expanded life in another, better world now seems impossible for the girl.

She collapses on the stone floor, sobbing beside a large crystal ball. Soon the ball begins to glow and within the glow the frightened girl perceives the face of her beloved Auntie Em all the way back in Kansas, frantically calling her name. "I'm here!" Dorothy cries. "In the witch's castle!" But alas, Auntie Em seems unable to hear her lost niece.

The image fades and as Dorothy clutches at the last vestiges of her Auntie's face, another face looms out of the darkened glass: the ugly, green face of the witch, who mocks her. "Auntie Em, Auntie Em, come back!" the witch cackles cruelly. "I'll give you Auntie Em, my pretty!"

And here, doomed and alone, without friends or any hope of escape, Dorothy is in the Dark Night of the Soul, that part of the Hero's Journey that Campbell called the Belly of the Whale. It is often described as a person's lowest point of the journey, yet it is also here that the deepest understanding of one's true nature and soul's purpose are presented. By entering this stage, our hero shows a willingness to undergo metamorphosis. It is during the time in that long, dark night that the interior depths must be tapped even further in order to find the strength and inner resources to eventually emerge as the true hero.

How do we do this? We must rally physically, mentally, and spiritually to uplift ourselves, to escape from the doldrums and wade into the battles that life has in store for us. When mired down in your own Dark Night of the Soul, the first thing to do is to get your body moving. Shock your senses and get going! When in doubt, plunge your bare feet into the snow, so to speak; do something to wake yourself up and get moving in another direction.

Process: The Action Box

I suggest that you create an Action Box. You may choose to paint the box or cover it with a collage of colorful images that motivates you.

In this Action Box you should place a minimum of five real, physical things that are personal to you items that remind you to get moving and shift your consciousness when you are feeling especially discouraged. For example, your Action Box might contain a favorite

CD loaded with lively dance music, a swimsuit so that you can plunge into a local public pool (of new possibilities), a pen and journal to do a little creative writing or doodling, watercolors and heavy paper to paint yourself out of the darkness, or perhaps a DVD of Qigong exercises to align your breath with focused movement and awareness. You might put a camera in there so you can focus on interesting features of nature while you take a walk. So get moving! Ride a bike. Dig in the dirt and plant a garden. Beat a drum. Shake a rattle. Sing! When you're stuck, get up, get out, and do something entirely different with your physical body. Experience activities you have never done before. Go to the library and check out a book of Thai cooking and surprise your neighbors with a meal. Volunteer to assist someone in need. Nothing gets a person up and out of his or her own mental funk like helping others.

Next, create a shift internally. This may take some mental repro-gramming, since the media regularly bombards us with a barrage of hopelessness. Newspapers, radio, television, and the internet are overrun with stories proclaiming doom and destruction. Those who pour stories out through the media would have us believe that the world is a scary and violent place. New wars are breaking out; there is murder in the streets; a doomsday asteroid is coming; destructive viruses are immune to antibiotics; Viagra has been recalled, and on and on. It is all too much for our minds and our spirits to take, and this onslaught never seems to end.

Let me take a moment to give you some real news—good news involving one of the most unnerving stories above (no, not the one about Viagra). I am talking about our basic fear of war and violence. Believe it or not, we are living in a world that is becoming more peaceful. In fact, according to an article written by Joshua Goldstein, an

American University professor emeritus of international relations, despite conflicts in Afghanistan and Iraq,

> The last decade has seen fewer war deaths than any decade in the past one hundred years, based on data compiled by researchers Bethany Lacina and Nils Petter Gleditsch of the Peace Research Institute Oslo. Worldwide, deaths caused directly by war-related violence in the new century have averaged about 55,000 per year, just over *half* of what they were in the 1990s (100,000 a year), a third of what they were during the Cold War (180,000 a year from 1950 to 1989), and a hundredth of what they were in World War II. If you factor in the growing global population over the last century, the decrease is even sharper. Far from being an age of killer anarchy, the twenty years since the Cold War ended have seen an era of rapid progress toward peace.

> The last conflict between two great powers, the Korean War, effectively ended nearly sixty years ago. The last sustained territorial war between two regular armies, Ethiopia and Eritrea, ended a decade ago. Even civil wars, though a persistent evil, are less common than in the past; there were about a quarter fewer in 2007 than in 1990.

> If the world feels like a more violent place than it actually is, that's because there's more information about wars that comes to us, not an increase in the wars themselves. Once-remote battles and war crimes now regularly make it onto our TV and computer screens, in more or less real time. Cell-phone cameras have turned citizens into reporters in many war zones. Societal norms about what to make of this information have also changed. As Harvard University psychologist

Steven Pinker has noted, "The decline of violent behavior has been paralleled by a decline in attitudes that tolerate or glorify violence."[2]

So, when you find yourself in the throes of a Dark Night of the Soul, turn off all the media noise and go within. In my program for Social Artistry, we teach facilitators exercises to expand the senses. One of these is called Remembering Joy. It is possible—even while experiencing a Dark Night of the Soul—for your amazing mind to harvest remembered experiences of joy in your life and also to relive the sense of well-being they provided.

You are now going to give yourself the gift of time travel. The following exercise only takes a few minutes of clock time; however, those few minutes are equal to all the time you need. The more you play with time, the more you get a sense of how fluid your psyche actually is.

Having more subjective time gives you more time to rehearse and remember joy. Remembering joy opens you to better relationships, deeper understanding, and greater appreciation of life.

Process: Remembering Joy

Sit comfortably in a chair with your feet flat on the floor. Close your eyes. Breathe calmly and deeply in through your nose and out through your mouth several times. With each breath, feel your body relaxing more.

Remember an incident from your life that gave you considerable joy. Use all of your senses and imaginative faculties to live in that place of remembered joy as if you were still there. What do you see? Smell? Hear? Taste? How does your body feel? Set a timer and stay in that state of joy for two full minutes of clock time. When your two minutes are up, open your eyes.

How does it make you feel to remember joy? Was it easy or difficult for you to stay in the state of joy the entire time? How can remembering joy influence your day-to-day life?

Remembering joyful situations frequently throughout the day is a way to build a life of appreciation. I find that when I'm really down in the dumps, the practice of remembering joy gives me a truer perspective on my life. Too often we fall into the pattern of remembering only sorrows or painful moments. Focusing on negativity increases our sensitivity to pain and fixates us more intensely on whatever difficulty comes our way. By maintaining this pattern of pain we move from chronic hurt to cynicism to paranoia, and to thinking that the world "has it in" for us.

This process of remembering joy has quite the opposite effect. Try applying mindfulness to your thoughts. When an unhappy memory or toxic thought starts to cross your mind, say, "Stop!" and reframe that thought to one of remembered joy. If you can't quite do that, then try practicing gratitude for everything you have and everything you are. Before you go to bed at night, write down all of the good things that happened to you during the day. Write down all your blessings and pour out gratitude from your heart for these things. Gradually, you rebuild your mind into an Emerald City of light instead of the dark and gloomy castle of the Wicked Witch. The practice of gratitude for whatever the day brings reveals the side of life beyond the shadows.

Look around you right now. In this moment, what are you grateful for in your surroundings and your life? Is it the beauty of a plant, the sound of a friend's voice, or the sight of your children? Is it a pet curled up beside you? If you really want to change your life, and help improve the lives of others, commit yourself to practicing gratitude each day.[3]

Back in the Land of Oz we find that Toto has returned to the woods to find the Tin Man, the reassembled Scarecrow, and the Lion. The Scarecrow comprehends that the dog's frantic barking is really an urgent message as to the whereabouts of Dorothy. He urges the allies to follow the little terrier, who then leads them all back toward the castle. The friends scramble up the jagged, jutting rock walls and peer down upon the scene below. Night has fallen, and the castle is surrounded by fearsome guards who march in rigid, orderly patterns. Three guards spy them as they crouch low in their hiding place, and a scuffle breaks out. But the Scarecrow hatches a clever plan (not bad for having no brain).

Momentarily, the trio of allies disappears, only to reappear transformed, wearing the uniforms of the three guards they have temporarily knocked out. They sneak into the castle by following the line of heavily armed guards as they march across the drawbridge. The Cowardly Lion's tail, too long to be contained within the guard's coat, swishes back and forth nervously outside of it, while Toto brings up the rear to make sure that his friends get safely inside the castle.

The cairn terrier with the heart of several lions leads the rescuers up a stone stairway, and the Tin Man uses his trusty ax to chop down the heavy door to the room where Dorothy is being held prisoner.

"Oh hurry, please hurry!" Dorothy pleads through her tears. "The hourglass is almost empty!"

Once reunited, our heroes hurry back down the stairs and into the great entrance hall just as the massive doors to freedom swing shut with a resounding *CLANG!*

"Going so soon?" the witch calls from atop the stairs. Dorothy and her allies huddle together as the battalion of guards move in on them with razor-sharp spears at the ready. Ever fearless as the life force with four furry paws, Toto barks furiously at the mob. At the moment it seems as though our heroes may meet an untimely end after all, the Scarecrow gets another brilliant idea. He notices a rope tied off on the wall that leads to a great wooden chandelier that just happens to be hanging directly above the guards' heads. He grabs the Tin Man's ax, chops through the rope with a single blow, and sends the heavy fixture crashing down on the guardsmen.

This narrow escape is a good thing to recall when life gets you down. Always remember that your great allies of mind, heart, courage, and the life force itself are there to help you out of any predicament, even when time seems to be running out. Run, Toto, run! might be your motto whenever you need to send your life force out to bring these great inner allies—these powerful qualities you possess—back to help. Remembering these attributes, you can always find a way to move forward.

Now our heroes are running through the castle, upstairs and downstairs in a landscape reminiscent of an M. C. Escher painting. When one exit is cut off, they try another, until at last they are forced up to the castle's tower battlements. The witch has ordered her guards to split up, and now Dorothy and her friends are hemmed in on both sides, cornered and trapped. This time there is no escape. The witch rushes forward. "Well! Ring around the rosy, a pocket full of spears!" she croons. "Thought you'd be pretty foxy, didn't you? Well, I'm going to start in on you right here . . . one after the other."

Our friends are shaking in fear as the witch says to Dorothy with that most horrible of lines, "And the last to go will see the first three go before her! And your mangy little dog, too!"

The Wicked Witch spies a torch burning brightly on the wall and smiles. She holds her broom up to the flame, and it ignites. "How about a little fire, Scarecrow?" she shrieks with delight as she sets his raised straw arm on fire.

Our kind and floppy friend's worst fear is realized, and he cries out in horror, "I'm burning! I'm burning! Help!" Thinking only of saving her beloved friend, Dorothy instinctively grabs a nearby bucket of water and tosses the water on the flames consuming the Scarecrow's arm. This water of life also douses the witch accidentally. The evil creature hisses and screams as the liquid soaks her and, amazingly, she begins to melt.

"Oh, you cursed brat!" she laments. "Look what you've done! I'm melting! Melting! Oh, what a world, what a world. Who would have thought a good girl like you could destroy my beautiful wickedness!?" The water of life is poison to her evil system, and she continues to steam and melt, screeching all the while as she dissolves and shrivels from sight.

And what does this tell us? Bring the water of life into any situation and the old decaying institutions cannot maintain their dusty structures. How would you bring water to the dusty structures of education, health, local government, and other issues that concern you? How might we pour life-giving and soul-stirring water on outmoded situations?

The Wicked Witch is gone, melted into the floor. Her broomstick lies next to her iconic pointed hat. The guards move in to look at what is left of their mistress. Dorothy and her allies have no idea what to expect. Will the legion of guards attack and devour them? Then the leader of the guards speaks. "She's dead! You've killed her!"

Our compassionate hero points to the Scarecrow. "I didn't mean to kill her, really I didn't." And we know this is true. She was just trying to save her friend.

The leader of the guards turns to his men. "Hail Dorothy! The Wicked Witch is dead!" Rather than persecute her, the soldiers honor Dorothy, setting her free and happily giving her the witch's broomstick.

Returning to the glorious Emerald City in triumph, Dorothy and her group present the Wizard with the broomstick. "Please, sir." Dorothy smiles. "We've done what you told us. We've brought you the broomstick of the Wicked Witch of the West. We melted her."

"Ah," the Wizard booms. "You liquidated her, eh? Very resourceful."

When Dorothy asks the great Wizard to grant their boons, he backpedals, telling the heroes to come back the next day. Although they have performed every impossible task to perfection, he refuses to grant their wishes, and with much bluster, fire, and smoke, bellows at them to leave. They all protest and begin to argue with the Wizard.

Where once the young girl was humble and meek, Dorothy has now found her inner strength and her voice. "If you were really great and powerful, you'd keep your promises!" she insists. In the Hero's Journey, this is known as Apotheosis, when the hero's old limited self dies and is transformed into a new being of light, divine knowledge, love, and compassion. Dorothy now is clearly much more than the girl we met in Kansas.

At that point Toto trots over to a heretofore unseen screen and draws back the curtain there to reveal an ordinary mortal man speaking into a microphone, shifting gears and pulling levers to create special effects. It is the Wizard himself without the garb of his illusions. Flustered at being found out, the Wizard shouts into the microphone, "Pay no attention to that man behind the curtain! Go before I lose my temper! The Great and Powerful Oz has spoken."

But of course, everyone has seen him in all his undignified poses, pulling the gears, shouting, and looking found out. Dorothy marches right up and scolds him, "You're a very bad man."

"No, my dear," he insists, "I am a very good man. I'm just a very bad Wizard."

The Scarecrow demands that the man make good on his promise to send Dorothy home, to give the Tin Man a heart, and to give the Lion his courage. The Tin Man reminds the humbug Wizard that he also promised the Scarecrow a brain.

"Well—I—but you've got them. You've had them all the time," the man stutters.

"You promised us real things," the Scarecrow says. "A real brain!"

"A real heart!" says the Tin Man.

"Real courage," the Lion intones.

Then, an incredible thing happens. The Wizard in human clothing smiles and seems wise and is eloquent when he says, "Boys, you're aiming low. You not only surprise, but you grieve me." He turns to the Scarecrow.

Anybody can have a brain. That's a mediocre commodity. Every pusillanimous creature that crawls on the earth or slinks through the slimy seas has a brain. Back where I come from, we have universities—seats of great learning—where men go to become great thinkers. And when they come out, they think deep thoughts, and with no more brains than you have. But they have one thing you haven't got, a diploma!

The Wizard opens a secret cabinet and pulls out a large velvet bag and from that come several diplomas. Selecting one, he hands it to the Scarecrow. "Therefore, by virtue of the authority vested in me by the Universitatus Committeeatum E Pluribus Unum, I hereby confer upon you the honorary degree of ThD—Doctor of Thinkology!"

The Scarecrow's brain swells with happiness, and he thanks the Wizard profusely. Next the man motions the Lion forward saying,

You, my fine friend, are a victim of disorganized thinking. You are under the unfortunate delusion that simply because you run away from danger you have no courage. You are confusing courage with wisdom. Back where I come from we have men who are called heroes. Once a year, they take their fortitude out of mothballs and parade it down the main street of the city. And they have no more courage than you have. But, they have one thing you haven't got, a medal!

The Wizard produces a shiny medal from out of the velvet bag and pins it to the Lion's chest, declaring, "Therefore, for meritorious conduct, extraordinary valor, conspicuous bravery against wicked witches, I award you the Triple Cross. You are now a member of the Legion of Courage!" The Wizard leans forward and kisses the Lion on both cheeks, and our brave feline is speechless.

Turning to the Tin Man the Wizard says,

As for you, my galvanized friend, you want a heart! You don't know how lucky you are not to have one. Hearts will never be practical until they can be made unbreakable. I could have been a world figure, a power among men, a successful wizard, had I not been obstructed by a heart. Back where I come from there are men who do nothing all day but good deeds. They are called philer—phil—er, uh good-deed-doers. And their hearts are no bigger than yours. But, they have one thing you haven't got! A testimonial!

With this, the Wizard pulls another object out of the velvet bag, a heart-shaped watch, which he presents to the Tin Man. "Therefore, in consideration of your kindness, I take pleasure at this time in presenting you with a small token of our esteem and affection. And remember, my sentimental friend, that a heart is not judged by how much you love, but by how much you are loved by others."

Thus the Wizard, in a kind of example of brief psychotherapy, bequeaths the external sign of the quality that each of the allies has already demonstrated. Psychoanalyst David Magder has suggested:

> The Scarecrow, the Tin Man, and the Cowardly Lion represent syndromes with which most therapists are familiar: low self-esteem based on the sense that one is not intelligent or capable of dealing with the world as one would like to, or a sense of inability to respond emotionally or effectively, and anxiety or fearfulness in dealing with the day to day problems of living.[4]

So, what do they do but seek therapeutic help from the Wizard. When the Wizard sends them through various therapeutic procedures, which each accomplishes successfully, he effectively concludes his psychotherapy by pointing out that all they lacked was belief in themselves, and through their actions have already demonstrated the very qualities they imagined they were lacking. In giving them artifacts of these qualities—a degree, a ticking heart, and a medal—they are immediately cured. Not a bad psychotherapy at all.

The three of them are delighted and proud, but Dorothy looks sadly at the Wizard and says, "I don't think there's anything in that black bag for me."

"Child," he cries, "You cut me to the quick. I'm an old Kansas man myself . . . born and bred in the heart of the Western wilderness." The Wizard promises to personally take her back to the land of "E Pluribus Unum" (in the Many there is the One), for many years ago he flew up in a runaway hot air balloon from the Omaha State Fair, and that is how he, too, landed in Oz.

The Wizard and former balloonist promises to take Dorothy back with him, leaving the people of Oz in the capable hands of their new leaders, the Scarecrow, the Tin Man, and the Lion. Dorothy tells each one good-bye tenderly, kissing them and brushing away their tears.

Yet once again, our hero's plans are thwarted. Just as Dorothy and the Wizard are about to rise into the stratosphere, Toto growls at a cat and leaps from the girl's arms. The girl jumps out of the balloon's basket to retrieve her dog just as the balloon without ballast begins to lift off without her. The Wizard cannot come back to get her, for fate has been set into motion, and he is unable to stop the rising balloon. As he flies up and up into the air, he cries down at her, "I don't know how it works!"

As the hot air contraption heads off and away from Oz, Dorothy is crestfallen. "Now I'll never get home!" she laments. Apparently, there is yet one more lesson to be learned along this Hero's Journey, for we have arrived at what Joseph Campbell calls the Ultimate Boon, where our hero achieves the goal of her quest. In some mythic stories, the Boon takes the form of an elixir of immortality or even the Holy Grail. For Dorothy, the Boon is simply a way to get back home. It is at this point that the forces of deep Nature, the forces of true and totally unexpected good, can intervene. For a third time, Glinda the Good Witch of the North appears in a bubble of light.

"Oh, will you help me? Can you help me?" Dorothy begs the Good Witch.

"You don't need to be helped any longer," Glinda says. "You've always had the power to go back to Kansas."

"Why didn't you tell her before?" the Scarecrow asks.

"Because she wouldn't have believed me." Glinda smiles, "She had to learn it for herself."

The Tin Man has to ask, "What have you learned, Dorothy?"

The girl from Kansas addresses her friends. "Well, I think that it wasn't enough just to want to see Uncle Henry and Auntie Em, and it's that if I ever go looking for my heart's desire again, I won't look any further than my own backyard. Because if it isn't there, I never really lost it to begin with. Is that right?"

Glinda happily confirms, "That's all it is." Dorothy sees that her power arises from within herself. Glinda reveals the secret of the ruby slippers by telling Dorothy that all she has to do is close her eyes, click her heels together three times, and intone the sacred mantra, "There's no place like home. There's no place like home."

Saying her final good-byes, the fully empowered Dorothy closes her eyes and clicks the heels of her sparkling ruby slippers together while repeating the words that will send her across the dimensions of time and space in a whirl of spinning images to return as the Master of Two Worlds. When she opens her eyes in Kansas, she is still whispering her heart's belief, "There's no place like home." She finds herself in her own bed in the tornado-torn, monochrome room of her farmhouse.

In Campbell's terms, this is called the Crossing of the Return Threshold, where our hero requires a guide or assistant to bring her back to her everyday life. We see such a loving guide in the form of Dorothy's own Auntie Em.

Just as she sits up and realizes where she is, Professor Marvel sticks his head in the window. "Anybody home? I just dropped by because I heard the little girl got caught in the big—" He smiles at Dorothy. "Well, she seems alright now." Uncle Henry steps into the room along with farmhands Hunk, Hickory, and Zeke (the earthly equivalent of her magical allies in Oz played by Ray Bolger, Jack Haley, and Bert Lahr, respectively). They arrange themselves around Dorothy in a circle, almost like a Renaissance painting of the last supper—suggesting completeness and perfection.

"She got quite a bump on the head," Uncle Henry announces. "We kinda thought there for a minute she was going to leave us."

"But I did leave you, Uncle Henry, that's just the trouble," Dorothy tells the group. "And I tried to get back for days and days."

"There, there, lie quiet now," Auntie Em soothes, pushing Dorothy down on the bed. "You just had a bad dream."

"No," Dorothy sits up again. "It wasn't a dream; it was a place." She points to the farmhands. "And you, and you, and you—" she points to Professor Marvel—"and you were there." She recognizes them all, having met their archetypal selves in Oz. The girl continues to insist that she really did visit a beautiful place somewhere over the rainbow, and at last turns to the dog on her lap, "Oh, but anyway, Toto, we're home!"

Part of Dorothy's experience was scary: she left Kansas on the back of a twister, found herself in a world where none of the normal rules applied, and was hunted by an evil witch. Yet she also met her entelechy, the Great Friend, in Glinda, and had magical allies join her on an adventure that changed her life and her way of being. Through it all, she stood in her integrity, did what came naturally to her, and became much more than she ever could have imagined. The girl returned from Oz in the profoundly matured condition of one who has undergone a full initiation embodying the realm that lies over the rainbow, the deepened and extended land.

Dorothy looks around at the warm faces in the room and tears come to her eyes as she says, "Oh, Auntie Em, there's no place like home!"

At last we have reached the final step on Campbell's Hero's Journey, known as Freedom to Live. Our hero has returned as the Master of Two Worlds and may now move beyond the fear of death to live as one who truly lives in the moment, neither anticipating the future nor regretting the past.

Throughout the story Dorothy, as the Possible Human, is seen as the building block of the possible society. The metaphor of this story applies to both the personal and societal aspects of all of our lives. She returns changed; she has become mythic. She has undergone adventures that have helped her to discover the riches and uses of her own intelligence, the opening of the heart, friendship and compassion, and the courage that comes of taking risks and meeting all challenges. She has learned about the magic, the wizardry, the sacred potency that is contained within each of us. She not only accepts these deepened aspects of herself but she appreciates them. Dorothy has returned home as a grander version of herself to re-green the wasteland of Kansas with her newfound knowings. Though she feels she can find everything she needs "in her own backyard," the audience knows that the backyard includes the vaster domains of her subconscious mind, and quite possibly the collective unconscious of the human race and the planetary mind as well. She is ready and able to cocreate a beautiful new world that works for all.

10

THE WIZARD OF US

Dorothy returns to Kansas after her adventures in Oz as what Joseph Campbell described as "one who can walk between two worlds."[1] She has learned that she is much more than a frustrated farm girl; she is now a hero who has traveled far and risked everything, returning home as an entirely different person. And because Dorothy's journey is also your journey, you can understand, as she did, that we all carry everything we need inside of ourselves. We are the Scarecrow and the Tin Man and the Cowardly Lion, loaded with a fully activated brain, heart, and courage. We are Toto, the active life force, faithfully prodding us forward with gusto. We are also the naughty ones, the witches and the flying monkeys that swarm in occasionally to keep us sharp and keep things interesting.

We each have unlimited access to our own entelechy, that part of us that is the Great Friend who oversees, guides, and loves us. We each have an ability to read the mythic map, to find our life's compass rose, and understand the signs that guide us. We each can celebrate the fact that we already possess everything we need to create a burgeoning new Renaissance—a rebirth of self and society. Indeed, we need look no further than "our own backyards" to find the answers and energy we seek. The time has come for each of us to dare enter the inner sanctum of our own power, to stroll defiantly past all the smoke and mirrors in order to pull back the curtain and see who is really pulling all the controls and levers of our reality. We are creating it all. For the true Wizard is us.

Do you ever ask, *Why now, in all of human history, why am I here now?* The answer is that you are here now because you are needed more than ever. You specifically, bringing with you all of your unique perspectives, gifts, experiences, skills, and abilities. You have been called. You have heard the call and answered that call. You are here because the 13.7-billion-year experiment that has resulted in your life could readily come to an end within the next century. You are present at the birth of an opportunity that exceeds your imagination. Christopher Fry wrote, "Thank God, our time is now, when wrong comes up to meet us everywhere, never to leave us 'til we take the longest stride of soul we ever took."[2] You are an important part of this.

I believe you have been called to the material in this book. Your Great Friend the entelechy may have placed this book in your path. There is no question that you are being called to take initiatives that before would have seemed unlikely, if not downright impossible. But now the world has been rearranged, the reset button of history has been hit. And where before you knew yourself as a participant in gradual growth and even more gradual change, now your options have multiplied, as has the time factor increased from middling rapid to rampant expeditious. Your lifetime is now ten lifetimes long. And you no longer have the luxury of sloth. What is key here is that you understand your role as leader and Social Artist in this most compelling moment of human history, this new Renaissance on Earth.

Why a Renaissance? Because, when the time is ripe for renovation, that which is needed will arise from the soul of the world, the cosmic agenda, and the depths of ourselves to supply it. People grow laconic, bored, driven to outrage and hysteria if the impetus to newness and renewal goes too long wanting, too long waiting. Cultures fall into chaos. Economic and psychological depression, as well as violence, rule the day. But a Renaissance (from the Italian word *rinascita*) is literally a rebirth out of an outmoded, dying, or impossible situation. It is when the soul grows and becomes equal to the challenges, indeed, becomes able to lift and enlighten and offer new ways of being and doing.

Sometimes they say that genius is the way that some people find their way out of particularly desperate situations. When you consider what went before in the fifteenth through the early seventeenth centuries, it is well nigh miraculous that this occurred. From the dregs of the history of the fourteenth century arose an age in which—within the span of a single generation—Leonardo de Vinci, Michelangelo, and Raphael produced their masterworks; Columbus, Magellan, and Vasco de Gama discovered new worlds; Luther began the reformation; and Copernicus changed the way we look at the cosmos, centering ourselves on the sun, and thus began the scientific revolution. As Rick Tarnas said in his wonderful book *The Passion of the Western Mind*:

> Compared with his medieval predecessors, Renaissance Man appeared to have suddenly vaulted into superhuman status. Man was now capable of penetrating and reflecting nature's secrets, in art as well as science, with unparalleled mathematical sophistication, empirical precision, and numinous aesthetic power.

He had immensely expanded the known world, discovered new continents, and rounded the globe. He could defy traditional authorities and assert a truth based on his own judgment. He could appreciate the riches of classical culture and yet also feel himself breaking beyond the ancient boundaries to reveal entirely new realms. Polyphonic music, tragedy and comedy, poetry, painting, architecture, and sculpture all achieved new levels of complexity and beauty. Individual genius and independence were widely in evidence. No domain of knowledge, creativity, or exploration seemed beyond man's reach.[3]

With the Renaissance, life in the world seemed to hold an immediate inherent value, an excitement and existential significance that balanced or even displaced the medieval focus on an afterlife spiritual destiny. Humans no longer appeared inconsequential with regard to God, church, or Nature. There was an extraordinary proclamation of human dignity by the philosopher Giovanni Pico della Mirandola that on many fronts in diverse realms of human activity seemed fulfilled.

From its beginning in Italy with Petrarch, Boccaccio, Bruno, and Alberti, through Erasmus, Thomas Moore, Machiavelli, and Montaigne, to its final expressions in Shakespeare, Cervantes, Bacon, and Galileo, the Italian Renaissance did not cease producing new paragons of human achievement. In fact, you would not find, at least in the West, anything with regard to such a rapid development of culture and consciousness since the ancient Greek miracle at the beginning of Western civilization. It was a time of true rebirth. Above all else, it involved a change in perspective from everything that had gone before. Perhaps it is during Renaissance eras that we may actually be seeing the Mind of the Maker determining that the time has come for a major jump in culture and consciousness and inserting social and psychic enzymes to help effect these transitions.

Key to all of this is the Renaissance of Spirit, what I believe to be the single most important possibility for our time and ourselves. It is when we truly know ourselves as Godseeds ready to emerge into Godselves. Tapping into our inner Wizard and truly becoming a Renaissance person may be the single most important thing that we can do for life on Earth. It is now time to ignite and live from your spiritual depths. I want to inspire you to discover the genius of your larval mind. I want you to engage spiritual technologies—old and new—to explore the brave new worlds of the inner continents.

I invite you to become a superb catalyst, a carrier of a new genesis as the world is getting ready to move from chaos to Renaissance. I invite you to increase your spiritual income so that you have the wherewithal for the ethical and creative expenditures necessary for a Renaissance of Spirit. I invite you to hone the spiritual craft of soul making, one that illumines the journey as well as the art and discipline that leads to spiritual transformation.

This is as deep and profound a study of our double nature that ever there was—finite and infinite. For we are all Godseeds planted in a space-time vehicle, and thus always yearning, questing, drawn by the lure of becoming until we reach the destiny that has been guiding us all along. I want you to remember our original birthright and to commit again to following the path that leads us home to who and what we really are.

I want you to have a sufficiency of intellectual and moral passion to explore new ways of being for body, mind, and soul, and with it the ability to present the availability of an unobstructed universe both within and without. I want you to carry this illuminating life into the world and become a revelation to others, an intellectual and psychological beacon, an evocateur of new patterns, new relationships, and new discoveries. I want you to bring fresh mind and fresh matter to an old world and serve as a catalyst of change, a pathfinder of deeper realities to create a new Renaissance: a new Emerald City here on Earth. It is time for you to claim your role as a powerful Social Artist.

As Social Artists, how do we design a new Renaissance in which all may live with equality and equity in a world of our choosing? We have seen that the Italian Renaissance revisited and revitalized classic art and ideas from the early Romans and Greeks. The classics added new ways of thinking as people of that time began to expand as human beings and gain access to their depths. We can do this now. We can choose the best of what serves us and release all that which no longer serves us, such as war, injustice, poverty, hunger, and cruelty.

The Wizard of Oz has shown us how this transformation can begin right now. As we followed Dorothy on her journey, we saw that as she rose on a personal level, the society around her also rose. As she was reborn, the society was reborn to a higher vibration than that of the past. If we use only the past as our compass, we just re-create the past with all its problems. The new focus of the Oz that we create today is on the human being, the individual as part of an interwoven thread in the vast web of life so that we create a culture of true equality. This web includes all human beings: all women, children, elders, all ethnicities and economic levels—not just wealthy white men. Women are no longer tethered to a traditional place in society; they are the stewards of the land, of the family, and of our communities. They are essential agents of transformation.

To bring a new vision of the Possible Earth into reality, we need to begin with ourselves so that we are operating from the fullness of our being. Millions of people right now are experiencing a yearning to awaken to their unique gifts and offer them in service to the world while living a life of joy and fulfillment. It's a surging of the human spirit, a virtual global awakening on a scale that no one has ever seen before. Simply put, people are longing to finally feel fully alive and to fulfill their unique purpose in life. This may be difficult because our current social systems have not been set up to prepare us to live a life of true purpose. Today's culture exists not to nurture our highest aspirations, but to perpetuate the status quo. We need to move out of the small stories we have held about ourselves and the human race.

There is a saying that what the caterpillar calls the end of the world, the master calls a butterfly. This is butterfly time. Just as the guidance cells in the mush that is the caterpillar in its chrysalis suddenly begin to activate the transformation of mush into a butterfly, so, too, this is a time when we realize that the inherent codings or imaginal cells of our bodies, our communities and, yes, even of the planet are calling us to come together. We have the opportunity to form a lasting, interdependent civilization, one in which we live lightly on the earth; cross-pollinating cultures, ideas, and spiritual forms; and becoming transparent to transcendence. Butterfly time means we must rise out of the mush we've been caught in these many hundreds of years to take flight in the air of the new story that is emerging all around us. We must have the will and the willingness to discover our purpose, live a mythic life from the deepest core of our essence, and be an integral part of this extraordinary moment in history.

Let us explore the wavelength that seems to distinguish people whose highest aspirations appear to blossom in the world. It would seem that they are the ones who find the essential wave or stream and flow with it—their own particular Tao, as it were. This wave colors their moods and actions and brings appropriate beings, blessings, and opportunities into their stream from the shores of opportunity. To find this essential stream and gather its strength and purpose, it is often necessary to have had the experience of exploring many different streamlets before focusing on the essential one.

So, how do we find this stream? We find it on the archetypal or metaphysical level, through prayer and meditation and deepening into our own essence from which the stream or wavelength—the River of the Divine, which is both a calling and a gifting—enters the everyday life. We can recognize this by the sense of grace and delight that it brings. It fills the mind and heart with an enthusiastic yes!

Everything is available if we would just accept it. The issue seems to be one of receptivity. In other words, a new Emerald City (or Possible Earth) is truly in our midst, but we must live as if this were true; we must *believe* it. We must try to live *in* the new Emerald City and not in the outskirts. Living in this new way of being provides us with the appropriate abundance, ideas, and opportunities that the essential life requires if we are to live from the plan of our higher self, our inner Glinda, if you will.

One of the best ways of moving into this Possible World Made Real is to switch the heart's focus from the old ways of being to the new Kingdom of Oz, and then the mind will follow. Let me give you an example. Suppose you want to do something that would benefit this world, but either you feel blocked in its accomplishment, or you are making some progress, but your mind does not recognize it. What you must do is agree to your plan's natural resonance in the new Emerald City. Hold the belief that your achievement of this goal or desire already exists in archetypal reality. With a full heart, agree to its reality in the local world and be willing to receive it as a gift from Oz. If you feel the need for extra support in this, simply acknowledge and invite your Quantum Partner to participate in the process.

Quantum Partners are archetypes serving the larger possibility for your life and being in the world. As such, they can serve as the unique navigational instruments of your path, the tools you need to conduct life in the larger reality. Because if you have been operating from a sense of diminished existence or regret or an unhappy consciousness, you may need a mentoring force that is both within and without—that is, a human partner as well as your archetypal Quantum Partner. Whereas the one provides you with practical advice, support, and belief, the other offers you the gnosis and know-how of the larger field of reference. Both offer inspiriting and guidance. Together with these friends of space and time, depth and dimension, you begin to claim your unique purpose and potency in the world.

Whatever task or intention you have, place or project it into the construct of Oz, and commit yourself to it fully. As W. H. Murray wrote:

> Until one is committed, there is hesitancy, the chance to draw back, always ineffectiveness. Concerning all acts of initiative (and creation) there is one elementary truth, the ignorance of which kills countless ideas and splendid plans: that the moment one definitely commits oneself, then Providence moves, too. All sorts of things occur that would never otherwise have occurred. A whole stream of events issues from the decision, raising in one's favour all manner of unforeseen incidents and meetings and material assistance, which no man could have dreamed would have come his way. I have learned a deep respect for one of Goethe's couplets: Whatever you can do, or dream you can, begin it. Boldness has genius, power and magic in it.[4]

Begin to see your life as Ozified. As for the habits of doubt, regret, and despair, they cannot follow you into the new Emerald City. Release any numbness you may be holding and become alive again. It is out of your True Essence that the good things of life flow.

That being said, please know that this Possible World is deeply interwoven in the rest of the world—it is not really separate. Animals assume that the world works for them. Primal peoples assume that the world works for them, or that it did before the coming of colonization. Perhaps the myth of the biblical fall of human beings is the fall into forgetfulness, away from the instinctive pattern of the deep knowing of receptivity. The Fall allowed us to gain objective knowledge of how to live and work in the world. Our own falls in our lifetime give us vulnerabilities and empathies that add to our initiative and desire to make a better world.

Begin each day in the construct of Oz by quietly tapping into its high vibration—its special frequency of consciousness—before you even get out of bed in the morning. Check into this inner world throughout the day, and end your day there. Soon you catch its waves, its bell tones, more quickly and easily. You are able to call it up at will, and you begin operating out of a different wavelength, an expanded reality and perspective beyond your usual life and habits. You see each thing or person is seen in all of its possibilities. The gates between the worlds open. Remember that everything is frequency; everything is vibration; everything is energetic transfer. You might say that embodied resonance is essence. It is where entelechy meets reality-at-large. It is the place of optimal soul force and utter aliveness. It is the state where you and your Quantum Partner commune and are one. This building up of frequency is literally being in the flow, regularly being in contact and communion, the mythic life fully manifested in terms of consequence.

You maintain this condition through sacred time, sacred space, and sacred intention. Please remember that you are a station with many wavelengths and bandwidths. You may feel the attunement as electrical prickings, which suggests the grid in which we are encased and which assures contact and communication. It may take real work on your part before this becomes a habit, but as you know, you are naturally gifted in this with a heightened resonance system in your own body-mind.

Along the Yellow Brick Road of this journey into Oz we have learned to expand our brains and hearts and find the courage to move forward into the grandest version we dare imagine of the possible world. As newly activated beings, we stand ready to re-green the wasteland of our former lives and step into our roles as Wizards in a time in which our talents are very much needed. Nothing less than all of the magic at our command is required in this time.

We find ourselves entering into this great new Renaissance filled with the dynamic power of intention and the power of choice. Together, we are the ones who create this new Emerald City in which all may live in health, connection, and balance with each other and our world.

So, what does this better world look like to you? Perhaps we should put on our emerald glasses with their green lenses once again. Imagine what the new world might look like through this green lens; wearing them might allow us to see and create a sustainable and peaceful world differently and to see others differently as well.

The great divide between the very rich and the poor in America today is reminiscent of the times of the French Revolution, and we all know what happened then. Abject poverty not only encourages crime but also prompts people to numb their reality. Nearly half of nonviolent inmates in our nation's prisons are imprisoned on minor drug charges. We must, as a people, discover new ways of making our lives vital and potent without the need to medicate ourselves into a stupor. Imagine people turning off their television sets, tossing out the drugs and alcohol, and expressing themselves in original, creative ways that fire up their souls. Imagine the children being allowed to explore and experiment in the arts and sciences in schools without pressure to perform or engage in stress-producing competition for grades.

The new Renaissance requires exciting, relevant forms of education that spark and fuel passion in our young people. Imagine the kind of education that Dorothy would have had in Kansas: bleak and dry and as gray as the world around her. What is needed is a whole system of education that is cooperative, not competitive, and is based on real-life experiences, with initiations and tests that hone the spirit and abilities, that encourages the expansion of creativity and the imagination, that offers exploration in resourceful ways of solving problems and the overcoming of seemingly insurmountable odds.

Through our green lens of a Renaissance of Being, we might see a world where diversity is valued and where people work together to create sustainable housing, farming, alternative forms of energy, and transportation, thus creating more jobs and a stronger economy. It might be a place where justice, compassion, and tolerance are the prevailing constructs. This greening of our world might create a new green architecture such as that found in biomimicry.

People in this new Emerald City are eager to learn about cultures other than our own, which creates more compassion and understanding. We see each other in all of our fullness. The portrayal of women and men in the media is greatly expanded to reflect more than youth and beauty in formerly traditional, limiting roles. The elderly are seen as vital assets to the well-being of their communities: assisting in the raising of the children and honored for their life experience and wisdom. Birth is seen as a natural human function rather than a medical condition requiring all types of intervention. Death is also viewed as a natural part of our human journey, not something to be feared. People are supportive of local farmers and businesspeople. They work to keep themselves healthy with exercise and food that is not laden with chemicals.

A new Emerald City and a new world Oz must be a blend of our collective construct for the world we wish to inhabit, coming from a place of love and respect. Turn your emerald-green lenses on the world around you today and see the positive changes that are already taking place. In 1972, His Majesty the Fourth King of Bhutan, Jigme Singye Wangchuck, proposed that his country adopt a Gross National Happiness Index (GNH) in order to reflect a holistic approach that would take into account much more than mere economic achievement as the measurement of a country's success. Bhutan is a country located at the east end of the Himalayan Mountains, and shares borders with India and China. The people of this place are primarily Buddhist, and they outline their GNH philosophy with four pillars: fair government that serves the needs of its people (including job creation and reduction of the gap between the wealthy and the poor); socioeconomic development; cultural preservation (this includes knowledge of traditional folklore, language, and artistic expressions); and environmental conservation. The four pillars are broken down further to include categories such as psychological well-being, community vitality, cultural diversity and resilience, ecological diversity, health, education, and more, all of which are considered to be basic human needs. These things are actually measured through surveys in the urban as well as rural areas of the country as an indication of the GNH Index. It is believed in Bhutan that citizens thrive when spiritual and material developments occur in tandem.

In 2009, Jigme Thinley, the first democratically elected prime minister of Bhutan declared, "We know that true abiding happiness cannot exist while others suffer, and comes from serving others, living in harmony with nature, and realizing our innate wisdom and the true brilliant nature of our own minds." The idea of a Gross National Happiness Index put forth by the country of Bhutan is an inspiration that clearly illustrates what can be possible if we shift our focus away from purely economic considerations.[5]

We are the ones who can make this happen. The time has come to align our local selves with our mythic, limitless selves to unlock our greatest destiny. Each of us must decide what we want our lives to stand for, how we can uniquely contribute to a better world. We must think about our lives in terms of how we can live more fully, enhancing not only our own experiences but those of our families, our communities, and the planet as well. By thinking about what we can provide for the next generations rather than what we can horde for ourselves in this lifetime, we are choosing to create our own destiny instead of leaving our children's future up for grabs. Can we come each day from a place of beauty, energy, power, grace, passion and, most important, joy while we do our soul's work for the good of the whole? As Ellis Jones, Ross Haenfler, Brett Johnson, and Brian Klocke, authors of *The Better World Handbook*, told us:

> As a society we must reconnect to a set of values that reignite our collective humanity so that it burns bright within each of us. No society survives for very long without a moral compass to guide its evolution and progress, especially not one as powerful and rapidly changing as our own. We need to bring our values back onto center stage as a people. We must consciously choose a set of core values that every one of us can embrace despite our many differences—values like compassion, freedom, equality, justice, sustainability, democracy, community, and tolerance. Then we have to go about deliberately building our society as a place that increasingly reflects and nurtures the growth of these values in the world. We create this world by having each of us individually choose to live and act in ways that more closely reflect our own personal values and those values we share as a people. We must begin by creating a vision of a better world.

We can all imagine what a better world might look like—a world where peace, justice, compassion and tolerance prevail or where each person has more than enough food, shelter, meaningful work and close friends. Think about the world that you would like to live in. Let yourself imagine the possibilities of a world that you could be proud to leave for your children. What does a world look like with more love, acceptance, patience, understanding and equality? This vision of a better future will provide you with an inspiring goal to work toward and will keep your passion alive for the journey ahead.[6]

People all over the world are living out their vision for a better world. There is a global transformation occurring in which average people are increasingly open to making profound changes in the ways they live. Look at the changes you see around you in America and in your own community during the past few years: people are simplifying their lives, buying less stuff, working less, and giving back more to their communities. Concern and knowledge about the environment has spread for the last thirty years, while recycling has become a widespread habit. People are taking time to learn about other cultures and appreciate diversity. No matter where you turn, you see individuals doing their part in making the world a better place. You are not alone in building a better world. Anything we choose is possible.

This is the time for us to dig deeper, to do our inner work and bring together our minds, hearts, and courage. Look at new possibilities and proceed fearlessly. See a bigger picture. Expand the story.

The great German philosopher Hegel spoke about world historical individuals, people whose particular passions corresponded to the passion in the turnings of time who became the entrepreneurs of progress, the ones who truly made a difference. I believe that you can become one of them. How grand is your dream? You are the Universe in miniature, and this Universe is a work in progress, a state of continuous creation and cocreation with you. The Buddhists refer to it as interdependent co-arising—you and the Universe working together. This is also to say that the idea of separation between you and the Universe is an illusion.

Quantum physics has discovered something that mystics have long known: that our perception of the universe actually evokes the very universe that is observed. If we change the way we view the Universe, the Universe itself spontaneously reflects this change back to us, as the Universe is not separate from our perception of it. This means that our creative imagination is truly divine, in that it literally affects the very blueprint of reality. Our divine creative imagination is the part of us through which God or Cosmic Mind or the Universe imagines this world into being. Please remember that we live in a quantum universe of open-ended potential in each and every moment. We are partners in what is being dreamed up. How our Universe manifests depends on how we individually and collectively dream it into reality. Real power, then, is in the viewing—how we decide to experience the Universe. You are truly the Wizard of this new era on Earth.

So, knowing this, and having emerged fresh from Oz with a satchel of magic and limitless possibilities at your fingertips, ask yourself, *What do I choose to experience? What do I choose to create, and how can I make it happen?* My friend and longtime teaching associate Peggy Rubin and I created an effective thirteen-step Manifestation Plan to help you in achieving the next phase in your particular grand design. It follows the letters of the alphabet. Step into your role as a creative Wizard and make up your own steps for the last thirteen letters.

Process: Manifestation Plan

A   is for Altar. Create a sacred space, an altar for this intention. Dedicate both the altar and your work perhaps in the way that Buddhists do:

for the enlightenment of all sentient beings. Or whatever feels appropriate to you.

B   is for Blessing. Find some way of noting with appreciation all that has gone before, and create bouquets of gratitude for all that you have learned, seen, witnessed, and done. Place representations of this gratitude on your altar.

C   is for Call Out. State aloud your intention, your gratitude for the past, and your dedication. Find or create something that represents this intention. Place it in the center of your altar. Your statement may take the form of a prayer, or you may want to state the intention and then ask for that Great Source to assist you in manifesting the intention. Feed the words into your body energy as colors and fragrances and kinesthetic knowings, as well as resounding vibrational sounds. As time goes on, move the intention into present tense and hear the words as already accomplished.

D   is for Dedicated Discernment. Seek mentors or beings whose life work has felt similar to yours. Note the differences, if any, between them and you. From these differences, notice what you want to change or work with. Notice what you need. Take a personal inventory of those traits that will assist you in fulfilling your goals. Note the things you think will impede or stop you. Find other people who have managed to work through or transcend similar blocks and use their strategies to solve your own challenges. Ask for help in the subtle energy realms. Ask for help from the Great Source Energy to remove the impediments or burn through them. Place images of your mentors on your altar; read about them; study them. Whenever appropriate, use them as examples and act as they do or did.

Be willing to change the attitudes and beliefs you hold that hinder you from fulfilling your desired goal.

E   is for Envision and Enact. Create rich inner imagery of your task using all of your senses and your body's movement. What does your project look like? Smell like? Taste like? Feel like? Sound like? Add as many rich details as you can. Think about it from every angle. Picture yourself doing the work of each task through to completion. Engage all of your powers in imaging how the world will have changed and been enhanced by your work when the task is finished. See help of every kind coming to you and bringing to you everything that is needed. Feel the heavenly powers saying *yes!* to you because what you are creating is for the good of all. Concretize the images by putting in pictures or drawings of the world—and yourself—and when the task is finished, these images also go on your altar.

F   is for Focusing, Fuel for the Fire, and for Friends. Join a prayer group or a focus group with friends to work together on bringing in the Higher Power, and also for practical assistance. Friends can help to see you achieving things you may not have dreamed you could do. Hang in there with your desires. Be willing to shift and adjust your goal if need be. Boost each other's spirits. Know that the fires may be reduced to embers once in a while, but make sure they don't go out altogether. Pay attention to the things that feed your energy and to those things that drain you. Do more of the first and none of the latter. Place notes with your friends' goals on your altar alongside yours. Add things that keep you desiring and moving toward achieving your own goal.

G   is for Get Going Gracefully. Know that the journey itself is every bit as important as the accomplishment of your goal; it may, in fact, be the accomplishment. Tapping into both the left and the right sides of your glorious brain, use your favorite form—list-making, flow charts, mind maps, or gestalt-planning—to create a step-by-step plan. Know that unexpected adventures will pop up to change everything as you go along. Trust that the Great Power will use your energy and effort to create something more stupendous and more eternal than you dared dream; know that you will have visitations of grace as well as grit. Think about steps you can take every day, and take the first step now. Naturally, the plan goes on your altar. Notice how everything on your altar may change as time changes.

H is for Homework and Hang in There. The brain stays alive as we keep learning. What things can you learn that will help you achieve this intention? What studies call you that are related to your goal? What are things you want to know though they may seem completely unrelated to your goal but will keep you refreshed and surprised by joy on the journey? Keep a record of your learnings on your altar. Dedicate your studies to the same beings you have asked to assist you with your intention.

I is for Intensity. I heard a wise woman say recently that one of the purposes for the ancient tradition of adolescent initiation for girls was to prepare them to give everything when it was required. She was relating this specifically to giving birth, but I think it's applicable to all our lives. In our modern culture we are not trained to give everything— all of our attention, our absolute focus, our power, our willingness, our presence, our talent, our skill, our energy—for as long as it takes to get the job done. And we are not trained to do all of that with the knowledge that we might lose all in the process, but also knowing that the more we devote all that we have, the more alive we are in the moment. I think that may be why war has been so attractive in the past. Soldiers were trained to devote their all to the cause, while those at home felt that they were participating by giving their all to the cause as well. We need to train ourselves in such dedication without war. That takes practice. What is more worthy of your giving all than the next phase of your life's work? The unique expression of your soul's purpose? Give of yourself unstintingly and generously to your purpose.

J   is for Joy, Jokes, and Just Letting Go. Too much heavy seriousness spoils the journey to achievement. Too much attachment to the outcome skews the process to one of unremitting labor and vast efforts to push the river. Cartoons, jokes, and many moments of laughter also go into every meeting of your allies and friends, and on your altar. Cultivate a sense of physical joy in every step along the path and then send that joy to those around you.

K   is for Keeping Konscious while you Keep on Keeping On. Choose to spend more time in prayer consciousness or moment-to-moment, wide-awake awareness so that each decision has a new aliveness to it. Become more and more aware of how each choice you make in life sends out ripples that affect the world around you.

L   is for Lightness, Love, and Lingering Laughter. This twelfth step to getting where you want to be reminds you to dance through the process of creation with ease, generating more love for yourself as you go and basking in the love of others. In the process of moving toward your goals and remembering their purpose, your purpose, and the Highest Good, you meet many new people who may become friends. You generate new ideas and find so many things to chew on and delight yourself that when you finally arrive at your goal, you find yourself in a better, greener world.

M is for the Mind of God Made Manifest. The thirteenth step takes you to the place you have been aiming for. This is the place where the Mind of God has expressed itself through you, has been made manifest in a fresh and unique way. Celebrate! Make merry! You are doing amazing things.

Remember that you have support along the way. You need never feel alone in this soul work. Take the time to make connections that fill you and motivate you. So much can be accomplished through the establishment of teaching and learning communities. These action centers can become powerful pods for creation, instrumental in launching innovative transformations in health, education, the environment, social justice, creativity, partnership, and other issues. Gather with a team of others and let your imaginations go. Solve problems beyond cultural conditioning. Create something that has never existed before. Stretch beyond the boundaries of the familiar into uncharted territory. Hold a clear vision of what you want. This is how you can make a real difference.

Like Dorothy, you can flow with the winds of change rather than be buffeted by them. Loaded with spunk and ability, you can step out of your front door and onto the Yellow Brick Road of your own Grand Adventure where all things are possible. Your awakening is a gift to this world that needs you now more than ever. What will you do with your marvelous brains, heart, and courage? You are the Wizard, the Creator, the Orchestrator. You are the hero of your own mythic journey.

• • • •

Care to join us? Visit jeanhouston.com for more information on how you can be a part of creating a new Renaissance, a joyous and brilliant society, and a sustainable Earth.

ACKNOWLEDGMENTS

It began with laughter. My good friend Diane Nichols, the playwright, and I were recalling the time years ago when I created a seminar called The Possible Society and brought it to seventeen cities and many thousands of participants. I used the story of *The Wizard of Oz* as the theme upon which to weave all manner of processes to enhance the mind, heart, and courage of both people and communities. I recalled how in Norman, Oklahoma, someone brought her giant Irish wolfhound to play the part of Toto. The big dog spied a cat, and the ensuing chase made the hotel where we were giving the seminar look like Kansas after the fictional twister struck. Then there was the time when, dressed in straw as the Scarecrow, I briefly caught fire, and the bucket of water meant for me missed and thoroughly doused the mayor of the town (the name is best forgotten).

The inherent wizardry of the story did its magic, however, as the seminar inspried hundreds of projects, not the least of which were cleaning up the beaches of Santa Cruz, California; delivering dental care to the elderly and indigent in Oklahoma City, Oklahoma; and creating green-dollar communities in British Columbia, Canada, in which a portion of the profit from the sale of certain items remained in the community to be channeled into development. Thousands of social projects, many of them quite innovative, grew out of these Possible Society weekends, and many of the resultant groups have transformed over the years and continue to meet.

Subsequently, Diane Nichols became the in-house editor of this book, offering her high craft, hilarity, and wisdom to its unfolding. Richard Cohn, who has to be the most soulful publisher in the business, championed my vision and helped me bring this book to fruition. Thanks, too, to Michele Cohn for her encouragement and research assistance over the past two years. Great thanks are due to Oregon's finest artist, Denise Kester, for her painting "Mother Nature" as the cover on this book. My canny and energetic agent Bill Gladstone brought his unending skills to finding just the right publishing house, and I am ever grateful for the gift of his follow-through.

The Beyond Words staff and the Atria Books production staff are wonderful partners. Thank you, Gretchen Stelter, for your informative reader's report, and Anna Noak, for being the developmental editor. I so enjoyed our creative conversations and help in articulating the book's themes. Managing Editor Lindsay Brown was truly masterful in shepherding the book through copyediting and production, as were Linda Meyer, the copy editor; Emmalisa Sparrow and her editorial research skills; Bill Brunson, the typographer; and Devon Smith, the designer.

Special thanks to my business partner, Connie Buffalo, who brought her enormous skills, care, and native wisdom to the birthing of this book.

Like Dorothy, I have been gifted with a "backyard" of friends and coworkers who are true Wizards and who made the journey so delightful.

NOTES

All dialogue and quotes throughout this book are from the 1939 film version of this tale.

The Wizard of Oz, directed by Victor Fleming (1939; Culver City, CA: Warner Bros. Family Entertainment, 1999), DVD.

All music lyrics throughout this book can be found in Harold Arlen's *The Wizard of Oz: 70th Anniversary Deluxe Songbook*, lyrics by E. Y. Harburg (Van Nuys, CA: Alfred Music Publishing, 2009).

Foreword

1. Freeman Dyson, *Infinite in All Directions: Gifford Lectures Given at Aberdeen Scotland, April-November 1985* (New York: HarperCollins Publishers Inc., 1989), 117.
2. David Bohm, "David Bohm Quotes," ThinkExist.com: http://thinkexist.com/quotation/in_some_sense_man_is_a_microcosm_of_the_universe/327162.html.

Chapter 1

1. Joseph Campbell, *The Hero with a Thousand Faces* (Princeton, NJ: Princeton University Press, 1973).

2. Ibid., 97.
3. Ibid., 246.
4. Rebecca Loncraine, *The Real Wizard of Oz: The Life and Times of L. Frank Baum* (New York: Gotham Books, 2009).
5. Ibid., 160.
6. Kathleen Krull, *The Road to Oz: Twists, Turns, Bumps, and Triumphs in the Life of L. Frank Baum* (New York: Alfred A. Knopf, 2008), 31.
7. Loncraine, *The Real Wizard of Oz*, 172.
8. Krull, *The Road to Oz*, 34.

Chapter 2

1. L. Frank Baum, *The Wonderful Wizard of Oz* (Chicago: George M. Hill Company, 1900), 12–13.
2. Salman Rushdie, "Out of Kansas," *The New Yorker* (May 11, 1992): 93.
3. Ibid.
4. "*dreams that you dare to dream, really do come true.*"   Harold Arlen, "Over the Rainbow," *The Wizard of Oz*, lyrics by E. Y. Harburg (Van Nuys, CA: Alfred Publishing Co., 1939), 2.
5. A. H. Maslow, "A Theory of Human Motivation," *Psychological Review* 50, no. 4 (1943): 370–396.

Chapter 3

1. Rebecca Loncraine, *The Real Wizard of Oz: The Life and Times of L. Frank Baum* (New York: Gotham Books, 2009), 176.

Chapter 4

1. "*only had a brain.*"   Harold Arlen, "If I Only Had a Brain (If I Only Had a Heart) (If I Only Had the Nerve)," *The Wizard of Oz*, lyrics by E. Y. Harburg (Van Nuys, CA: Alfred Publishing Co., 1939), 1.
2. Norman Doidge, *The Brain that Changes Itself: Stories of Personal Triumph from the Frontiers of Brain Science* (New York: Penguin Books, 2007).
3. Ibid., 46–47.

4. Ibid., 47.

5. Ibid., 85.

6. Rick Hanson, *Buddha's Brain: The Practical Neuroscience of Happiness, Love, and Wisdom*, with Richard Mendius (Oakland, CA: New Harbinger Publications, Inc., 2009).

7. Rick Hanson, "Self-Directed Neuroplasticity: A 21st-Century View of Meditation," *Noetic Now*, 9 (April 2011): 1: http://noetic.org/noetic/issue-nine-april/self-directed-neuroplasticity/.

8. *"why the ocean's near the shore,"* Arlen, "If I Only Had a Brain," 2.

9. Hanson, "Self-Directed Neuroplasticity," 1.

10. Ibid.

11. Ibid., 2.

12. Ibid., 4.

13. Ibid.

14. Deepak Chopra quote from a Summoning the Sacred workshop, conducted with author (actual date unknown).

15. Alert Einstein, "Albert Einstein: Quotable Quote," Goodreads: www.goodreads.com/quotes/59688-i-think-that-only-daring-speculation-can-lead-us-further.

16. James M. Robinson, ed., The Gnostic Gospel of Thomas, saying 113, *The Nag Hammadi Library*, revised edition (San Francisco: HarperCollins, 1990).

17. Duane Elgin, *The Living Universe: Where Are We? Who Are We? Where Are We Going?* (San Francisco: Berrett-Koehler Publishers, Inc., 2009), 11.

Chapter 5

1. *"only had a heart."* Harold Arlen, "If I Only Had a Brain (If I Only Had a Heart) (If I Only Had the Nerve)," *The Wizard of Oz*, lyrics by E. Y. Harburg (Van Nuys, CA: Alfred Publishing Co., 1939), 3.

2. Rebecca Loncraine, *The Real Wizard of Oz: The Life and Times of L. Frank Baum* (New York: Gotham Books, 2009), 176.

3. Susan Steinbrecher and Joel B. Bennett, *Heart-Centered Leadership: An Invitation to Lead from the Inside Out* (Memphis, TN: Black Pants Publishing, 2003), 147.

4. Ibid., 147.

5. Ibid., 159.

6. Joyce Marley, "The Heart in Chinese Medicine," Acupuncture Services of Center NY, http://www.acupuncture-services.com/basic-theory/chinese-medicine-diagnosis/the-heart-in-chinese-medicine.php.

7. "36 Interesting Facts About . . . the Human Heart," Random Facts (January 28, 2010): http://facts.randomhistory.com/human-heart-facts.html.

8. Peter Walker, "Sleeping for Less than Six Hours May Cause Early Death, Study Finds," *The Guardian* (May 5, 2010): www.guardian.co.uk/society/2010/may/05/sleep-study.

9. Sleep Disorder, "Sleep Disorder Research: The Brain's Response to Lack of Sleep," Sleep Disorders Info.org: http://www.sleepdisordersinfo.org/200/sleep-disorder-research-the-brains-response-to-lack-of-sleep/ (accessed September 27, 2012).

10. Clarissa Pinkola Estes, *The Joyous Body: Myths and Stories of the Wise Woman Archetype/The Dangerous Old Woman, Volume III* (Boulder, CO: Sounds True, 2011), audiobook, 6 compact discs; 12 hrs.

11. The Pachamama Alliance, "Awakening the Dreamer Symposium" (embedded video), Transformative Workshops, Pachamama.org, www.pachamama.org/workshops/awakening-the-dreamer-symposium.

12. Eric McLamb, "The Ecological Impact of the Industrial Revolution," *Ecology*, September 18, 2011, http://www.ecology.com/2011/09/18/ecological-impact-industrial-revolution/.

13. "Current World Population," Worldometers: Real Time World Statistics, http://www.worldometers.info/world-population/ (accessed September 21, 2012).

14. InfiniteEarth, *Beyond Carbon, Beyond Sustainability: Introducing the Worlds First Fully Certified REDD++ Project: Rimba Raya Biodiversity Reserve* (Hong Kong: InfiniteEarth, 2010), 6.

15. Ahmed Djoghlaf, "Message from Mr. Ahmed Djoghlaf, Executive Secretary, on the Occasion of the International Day for Biological Diversity," Convention of Biological Diversity, http://www.cbd.int/doc/speech/2007/sp-2007-05-22-es-en.pdf (accessed September 21, 2012).

16. Marsha Walton, "Study: Only 10 percent of big ocean fish remain," CNNTech (May 14, 2003): http://articles.cnn.com/2003-05-14/tech/coolsc.disappearingfish_1_industrial -fishing-fish-numbers-longlines?_s=PM:TECH.

17. "National Survey Reveals Biodiversity Crisis—Scientific Experts Believe We Are in Midst of Fastest Mass Extinction in Earth's History," American Museum of Natural History, 2007.

18. "Environment Programme," United Nations Office for Partnerships: http://www.un.org/partnerships/environment.html (accessed September 21, 2012).

19. Drew Dellinger, "Hieroglyphic Stairway," *Love Letter to the Milky Way* (Ashland, OR: First White Cloud Press, 2011), 1; see also http://drewdellinger.org/.

20. E. F. Schumacher, *A Guide for the Perplexed* (New York: Harper & Row, 1977), 140.

21. Trevelen Rabanal story from author interview, April 4, 2012.

22. Debbie Kahn story from author interview, April 6, 2012; see also Amman Imman, www.ammanimman.org.

Chapter 6

1. *"only had the nerve."* Harold Arlen, *The Wizard of Oz: 70th Anniversary Deluxe Songbook*, lyrics by E. Y. Harburg (Van Nuys, CA: Alfred Music Publishing, 2009), 3.
2. Julia Butterfly Hill, *The Legacy of Luna: The Story of a Tree, a Woman and the Struggle to Save the Redwoods* (New York: HarperCollins Publishers, 2000).
3. Katherine Lane Martin, *Those Who Dare: Real People, Real Courage . . . and What We Learn From Them* (Novato, CA: New World Library, 2004), 213.
4. Ibid.
5. Stephen Diamond, "The Light and Dark Side of Confidence, What Is Courage?: Existential Lessons from the Cowardly Lion," *Psychology Today* (April 28, 2011): http://www.psychologytoday.com/collections/201110/the-light-and-dark-side-of-confidence/what-is-courage-existential-lessons-the-coward.
6. Chris Fontana and Alison McCaffree story from joint author interview, April 6, 2012; see also www.global-visionaries.org.
7. Jan Sanders story from author interview, April 5, 2012.
8. Martin, *Those Who Dare*, 82.
9. *"the dreams that you dare to dream, really do come true."* Harold Arlen, "Over the Rainbow," *The Wizard of Oz*, lyrics by E. Y. Harburg (Van Nuys, CA: Alfred Publishing Co., 1939), 2.

Chapter 7

1. Jeremy Rifkin, "The Empathic Civilization," Ted Talk, (August 2010): www.ted.com/talks/jeremy_rifkin_on_the_empathic_civilization.html.
2. John Kenneth Galbraith, *The Affluent Society* (New York: Houghton Mifflin Company, 1958), 153.
3. Jacob Needleman, *Money and the Meaning of Life* (New York: Currency Doubleday, 1991).
4. Mark 12:17, *The Holy Bible: King James Version*.
5. Needleman, *Money and the Meaning of Life*, 268.
6. Ibid., 270.
7. Lewis Hyde, *The Gift: Creativity and the Artist in the Modern World* (New York: Random House, 2007), 70.
8. Annie Leonard, "The Story of Stuff (2007, Official Version)," April 22, 2009, YouTube: http://www.youtube.com/watch?v=9GorqroigqM; see also: http://www.storyofstuff .org/2011/03/14/story-of-stuff/.

9. Victor Lebow, "Price Competition in 1955," *Journal of Retailing*, XXXI (Spring 1955): 5–10; 42–44; see also http://www.ablemesh.co.uk/PDFs/journal-of-retailing 1955.pdf.
10. Margaret Mead, "UFO's—Visitors from Outer Space?" *Redbook Magazine*, vol. 143 (September 1974).
11. Mary Morrissey quoted from a telephone conversation with author, May 7, 207.
12. Ibid.
13. Hopi Nation Elders, "We Are the Ones We Have Been Waiting For," said at a meeting of Elders at Oraibi, Arizona, 2000, quoted in Charles L. Whitfield, Barbara Whitfield, Russell Park, and Jeneane Prevatt, *The Power of Humility: Choosing Peace Over Conflict in Relationships* (Deerfield Beach, FL: Health Communications, 2006), 12.

Chapter 8

1. *"out of the woods."* Harold Arlen, "Optimistic Voices," *The Wizard of Oz*, lyrics by E. Y. Harburg (Van Nuys, CA: Alfred Publishing Co., 1939), 1.
2. Kathleen Krull, *The Road to Oz: Twists, Turns, Bumps, and Triumphs in the Life of L. Frank Baum* (New York: Alfred A. Knopf, 2008), 39.
3. Albert Einstein, "Albert Einstein Quotes," Brainy Quote: http://www.brainyquote .com/quotes/quotes/a/alberteins130982.html.
4. Mary Bellis, "The Invention of Velcro®—George de Mestral," About.com Inventors: http://inventors.about.com/library/weekly/aa091297.htm.
5. Abigail Doan, "Green Building in Zimbabwe Modeled After Termite Mounds," *In Habitat* (December 10, 2007): http://inhabitat.com/building-modelled-on-termites -eastgate-centre-in-zimbabwe/.
6. William McDonough and Michael Braungart, *Cradle to Cradle: Remaking the Way We Make Things* (New York: North Point Press, 2002).
7. Elle MacKenna, "Green Roofs: Energy Saving and Much More," *HubPages* (April 1, 2007): http://ellemackenna.hubpages.com/hub/Green_Roofs_Energy_Savings.
8. Janine M. Benyus, *Biomimicry: Innovation Inspired by Nature* (New York: HarperCollins Publishers, 1997), 6–7.
9. Arthur Schopenhauer, "Arthur Schopenhauer Quotable Quotes," Goodreads: http:// www.goodreads.com/quotes/196118-a-sense-of-humour-is-the-only-divine-quality-of.
10. Gary K. Palmer, "The Power of Laughter," *Ensign* (September 2007): 32–35; see also www.lds.org.
11. Ibid.
12. W. S. Hamerslough, "Laughter and Wellness" paper presented, Southwest District of AAHPERD, Kahuku, Hawaii (June 22, 1995).

13. Norman Cousins, *Anatomy of an Illness as Perceived by the Patient* (New York: W. W. Norton & Company, 1979).
14. L. S. Berk, "Neuroendocrine and Stress Hormone Changes during Mirthful Laughter," *American Journal of the Medical Sciences*, 296, no. 7 (1989): 390–96.
15. K. S. Peterson, "A Chuckle a Day Does Indeed Help Keep Ills at Bay," *USA Today* (October 31, 1996): 10D; see also Berk, *American Journal of the Medical Sciences* 296, no. 7, 390–96.
16. Helen M. Luke, *Laughter at the Heart of Things: Selected Essays from Helen M. Luke* (Sandpoint, ID: Morning Light Press, 2001), 99.
17. Daniel H. Pink, *A Whole New Mind: Why Right-Brainers Will Rule the Future* (New York: Riverhead Press, 2006), 186–187.
18. Ibid., 187.
19. Ibid.
20. Ibid.

Chapter 9

1. Pierre Teilhard de Chardin, "Inspirational Quotes," Beliefnet: http://www.beliefnet .com/quotes/inspiration/P/Pierre-Teilhard-de-Chardin/We-Are-Not-Human -Beings-Having-A-Spiritual-Experie.aspx.
2. Joshua S. Goldstein, "Think Again: War, World peace could be closer than you think." *Foreign Policy* (September/October 2011). http://www.foreignpolicy.com/articles/2011/08/15/think_again_war?page=full.
3. Jean Houston Foundation, *The Social Artistry Facilitator's Manual* (Ashland, OR: privately published, 2004): 32.
4. David Magder, "The Wizard of Oz: A Parable of Brief Psychotherapy," *The Canadian Journal of Psychiatry / La Revue canadienne de psychiatrie*, vol 25 (Ashland, OR: privately published), no. 7 (November 1980): 564–568.

Chapter 10

1. Joseph Campbell, *The Hero with a Thousand Faces* (Princeton, NJ: Princeton University Press, 1973), 183.
2. Christopher Fry, *A Sleep of Prisoners* (New York: Dramatists Play Service, 1951), 62; see also www.greatfulness.org/poetry/sleep_of_prisoners.htm.
3. Rick Tarnas, *The Passion of the Western Mind: Understanding the Ideas that Have Shaped Our World* (New York: The Random House Publishing Group, 1991), 224.

4. W. H. Murray, "Not Always On," Elise.com quotes: www.elise.com/quotes/wh_murray_-_until_one_is_committed/.
5. "Gross National Happiness," The Centre For Bhutan Studies, Thimphu, Bhutan, www.grossnationalhappiness.com.
6. Ellis Jones, Ross Haenfer, Brett Johnson, *The Better World Handbook: Small Changes that Make a Big Difference* (Gabriola Island, Canada: New Society Publishers, 2007), 4.